Alan Fairweather worked in sales and customer service and did the job of a manager for fifteen successful years. He now spends his time running seminars and workshops, developing skills on how to handle problem people and situations and come out of it with increased confidence and improved results. He is also the author of *How To Make Sales When You Don't Like Selling*. For more information, visit www.themotivationdoctor.com

Also by available from How To Books

Managing Conflict in the Workplace
Developing Mental Toughness
Presenting with Power
How To Be a Motivational Manager
Coaching Skills for Leaders in the Workplace
Top Performance Leadership

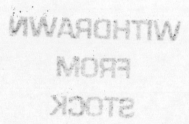

HOW TO MANAGE
DIFFICULT PEOPLE

Alan Fairweather

Constable & Robinson Ltd
55–56 Russell Square
London WC1B 4HP
www.constablerobinson.com

First published in the UK by How to Books Ltd, 2010

This edition first published by How To Books,
an imprint of Constable & Robinson Ltd, 2014

A copy of the British Library Cataloguing in Publication Data
is available from the British Library

ISBN: 978-0-71602-398-2 (paperback)
ISBN: 978-1-84803-438-9 (ebook)

1 3 5 7 9 10 8 6 4 2

Printed and bound in the EU

Contents

Preface   ix

1 **There's No Such Thing as Difficult**   1
People

It's What You Say   1

There Is a Solution   9

Identifying Difficult People   14

Do We All Have the Same Difficult People?   20

Why Are People Difficult?   22

Changing You or Changing Them?   25

2 **If You Don't Like the Programme**   27
– Change It!

First Impressions Count   27

Changing Your Behaviour   29

Using the Six Programmes of Behaviour   33

Inviting Programmes   39

Making the Right Choice   47

Self-fulfilling Prophecy   48

Deciding Your Default Programme   49

3   Build a Better Frame of Mind   52
Using the Five Factors of Success   52
1 Mind Control   53
2 Belief   61
3 Energy   66
4 Rapport   70
5 Courage   75

4   Prevention Is Better than Cure   80
Communicate on a Human/Business Level   81
Building Your Likeability Factor   86
Don't Get Hooked   90
Some Words Are Better than Others   92
Don't Let Pet Peeves Hook You   99
The Way You See It May Not Be the Way It Is   102

5   Choose to Be Assertive   106
Is Assertiveness Good or Bad   106
Exercising Your Rights   109
Being Responsible   111
You Choose   113
Assertiveness Techniques   117
Think Assertively   123

6   The Power of Persuasion   126
Developing Your Skills   126
It's About Change   133
Using Logic and Emotion   136
Selling Yourself   142
Planning Your Strategy   156
The Initial Approach   158

WIIFM   159
Dealing with Resistance   162
Principles of a Powerful Persuader   173

7 Strategies for Success   **175**
What Customers Really Want   175
Deal with Their Feelings – Deal with Their Problem   180
Reflective Listening   183
Using Empathy   184
Transition Steps   188
Visible–Voluble Concern   190
Managing Difficult Staff   192
Successful Leading and Coaching   195
The Good News   197
The Not So Good News   198
How to Coach   201
Using Your Customer Service Skills   203
Look for the Positive   204
The Truth about Staff Who Can't Perform   206
Summing Up   208

Index   **211**

Preface

Brain surgery – easy; rocket science – a walk in the park; air traffic control – simple! I doubt very much if any brain surgeon, rocket scientist or air traffic controller would agree with me on this, but I believe that managing people and particularly difficult ones is the hardest job in the world. No one shows you what to do, there are very few training programmes, and most people believe it is just something you can or can't do.

Frederick the Great once said: 'The more I get to know people, the more I love my dog.' For most of us, managing dogs is not an option; we have to manage people be they our staff, our customers, our colleagues or our nearest and dearest. The reason it's such a hard job is that every human being is different. Just because you successfully manage one in a particular way does not mean to say you'll be successful with others. Humans are the most complex and complicated pieces of equipment you'll ever have to deal with. Many of them have similarities but every one of them is different and they all work in a slightly different way. They are totally driven by their emotions and are unlikely to respond to any logical argument.

Every time I run a customer service, sales or management seminar we always have a section on managing difficult people. Of all the articles I've written and posted on the internet, managing difficult people and managing difficult staff are the most downloaded.

I spent 15 years as a manager dealing with staff and customers and I have the bruises to prove it. I understand the real challenge of managing difficult people and I've written this book to make life a little bit easier for others. There is no magic formula here, only some proven techniques for managing yourself and managing difficult people. If you gain a better understanding of yourself, build your confidence and use the techniques, then you'll make your life a whole lot easier.

I want to thank some of my buddies who helped me along the way. Dynamic Diane for her writer's input, and the occasional beer; John for his unvarying encouragement, and the occasional beer, and Linda for being there.

I wish you every success.

There's No Such Thing as Difficult People

IT'S WHAT YOU SAY

'Good morning, Bob, how are you today?'

'What's good about it, and why are you being so sarcastic? You know I'm up to my eyes in work and my back is really playing up.'

'I'm not being sarcastic; we're all busy and I don't know what's wrong with your back. I think you're just being grumpy.'

'Being grumpy! Do you know how much pain I'm in most of the time? It's alright for you, you don't have my problems!'

'You think you've got problems, Bob. Let me tell you a few things – you don't know the half of it!'

Does any of this sound familiar? Have you been involved in conversations like this? Who do you think is the difficult person here? I hear you saying: 'It's Bob – he's a grumpy old so and so'. But are you sure it's Bob who's being difficult?

Let's assume that you know Bob. He's 59 years old and hasn't kept well for a long time. He lost his wife a few years ago, he lives alone and he rarely sees any of his dispersed family.

Do you think 'How are you today?' was the best thing to say? In your mind, you were only being pleasant and 'How are you today?' is what you normally say to people you come into contact with. But perhaps you could have opened the conversation differently. You could have said something like:

'Good morning, Bob. I bet you're glad that football team of
yours had a win last night.'

It's not what you say to other people that matters, it's how they interpret what you say. I know that's difficult to get your head around, but it all depends on their map of the world. Say, for example, you compliment a colleague. You might say:

'Hey, you're looking really smart today – that suit looks great!'

They come right back at you with:

'What you're really saying is that I usually look a mess and it's
about time I tidied myself up.'

The problem you have here is that the person receiving the compliment may have low self-esteem. They probably believe that they look a mess most of the time and don't deserve a compliment. Perhaps they were brought up in a family where complimenting other people wasn't encouraged.

Some couples fall out because one of them puts their own spin on what the other person is saying:

'Sorry, Jill, I'm not able to visit your family this weekend.'

'What you really mean, Jack, is that you don't like my mother.'

'No, that's not what I mean. I have to work this weekend.'

'I bet you arranged that so you didn't have to see my mother!'

This may or may not be true, but perhaps Jack does have to work and Jill has totally misread the situation. Break-up and divorce may be on the horizon over a failure to communicate.

The other challenge you face is that human beings are totally driven by their emotions. Take the example above: Jack is stating quite logically that he has to work at the weekend. Jill, responding emotionally, feels that there is a hidden agenda. Of course, Jack may not like his mother-in-law, but that's not what this is about at this time.

Joe and Mr Smith

Let's listen in on a phone conversation between Steve, a business owner, and Joe, a customer rep, at one of his suppliers:

'Good morning, FDC Supplies. How can I help you?'

'How can you help me? I'll tell you how you can help me. You can get that order out to me that I placed with you last week. If it isn't delivered tomorrow, you can forget it!'

'What's your name and account number please?'

'My name is Steve Smith and I don't know my account number. My shop is called Smiths at 24 the High Street.'

'Hold on and I'll try and find your account from your name and address. How do you spell your name?'

'S-M-I-T-H! And could you get a move on, there are people in my shop waiting to be served.'

'I'm going as fast as I can but there are a lot of Smiths in our database.'

'Well, that's not my fault!'

'I've found it. According to my records, we don't have all the items in stock to complete your order.'

'Why didn't you tell me that when I placed the order – your service stinks!'

'It's not company policy to contact customers when we don't have items in stock. We told you that when you opened the account.'

'You did not tell me that. I want to speak to a manager.'

'You can't speak to the manager – he's in a meeting.'

I could go on with this, but I'm sure it's something you can relate to from either side of the conversation. So, who is the difficult person here? I'm sure that Joe would blame the customer for being unreasonable, aggressive, unpleasant and demanding. The customer may be all of these things, but, in this situation, Joe made it ten times worse! There are at least ten mistakes that Joe made with this customer. These mistakes added fuel to the customer's anger and made the whole thing much worse; it's like pouring petrol on a bonfire. This customer has probably been building up to this phone call. Perhaps he's under stress, business isn't going too well or there may be problems at home.

It's all in the mind

I'm reminded of the story about Tom the farmer, whose milking equipment broke down just as he was about to milk his cows. He remembered that his friend Sandy, who owned the next farm, had a portable milking machine. So Tom jumped in his Land Rover and headed down to Sandy's farm. As he was driving, he was thinking: 'I hope Sandy will lend me his machine – after all I've been a good friend to him. Maybe he won't want to lend it, which I think is a bit unfair; after all, I've lent him things in the past. I'm going to be really annoyed with him if he won't lend me the machine; after all, what have I ever done to him?' Tom got himself so worked up and, when he drove into Sandy's farmyard, Sandy called out:

'Good to see you, Tom, how are you today?'

'I'm fine, and you can keep your rotten milking machine. I never wanted to borrow it in the first place!'

Before people make contact with you, particularly an angry customer, a lot of other things could be going on in their mind. Those first few seconds with you will decide how long the anger continues. Anger doesn't really last that long – after about 20 seconds the anger chemicals start to subside. I'm sure you've heard the saying: 'Allow them to let off steam', and that often works. You've probably been in the situation where you ask your manager to phone an angry customer and suddenly the customer becomes Mr Nicey-Nicey!

In the Joe and Mr Smith case, the customer isn't handled well and the anger continues and gets worse. If Joe had used some different techniques and better words, he could have made life much easier for himself, never mind the customer. He wouldn't necessarily have turned this customer into 'Mr Nicey-Nicey' but he could have poured some cool water on the bonfire and defused the customer's emotions.

Of course, we can't tell from the dialogue above what Joe's tone of voice was like or his body language. And before you write to me, body language does matter over the telephone! I was listening to the radio while driving one day. The presenter was running a phone-in competition and a contestant called Wendy was on the phone. There was the usual preliminary chat: where are you from and what do you work at sort of small talk. Wendy said that she worked in the customer service department of a large insurance company, dealing with clients on the phone. It was so apparent from her tone of voice that Wendy was a warm and friendly person – you could hear her smiling down the phone. At one point the presenter said, 'Wendy, if I ever phoned your company to complain about something, I'd probably forget all about it within minutes of speaking to you.'

Joanne and the Boss

'Joanne, could you get the board report finished for me tonight.'

'It'll take me a couple of hours and I was hoping to get away on time tonight.'

'I appreciate that, Joanne, but I really need that report tonight.'

'Could you ask Susan to do it, I know she wouldn't mind.'

'I'd prefer you to do it, Joanne, because you always do it better than anyone.'

'I promised my husband I'd be in on time tonight, because we want to go out later.'

'I understand that, Joanne, but in these difficult times we all have to put in a bit more effort. You know it won't take long and I'd really appreciate it.'

Here we have a manipulative boss who's giving no thought to Joanne's needs. Nevertheless, Joanne could have handled this situation much better by being a bit more assertive. Now I realise you may be thinking, 'You have to do what your boss wants and if you stand up to them then you'll only make life more difficult for yourself.' It's true to say that you won't always win, but I'm going to show you what to say and what to do in order to make life easier for you in this kind of situation. It's not a case of standing up to your boss; it's a case of communicating your needs and still getting the job done.

We all get stressed

I'm sure you can relate to all of these situations, from either side of the fence. They make life difficult, they contribute to stress and all the negative consequences of that. Dealing with other people is one of the main causes of negative stress. I continually hear comments such as:

'Why does he want me to do that?'

'How am I supposed to know what she's thinking?'

'Why do they behave like that?'

We can get extremely stressed when people don't see things the way we do. Let me make something really clear: other people don't see things the way you do, or the way I do, and they might never do.

Every human being in this world is different from each other; we're all as different as our fingerprints. Some of us are very similar and that's why we become friends with some people and even share our lives with them. However, as you well know, even your closest friends and the person you share your life with still see the world differently from you. Your customers, staff, boss and colleagues see, hear and experience situations in different ways from you. They're not necessarily doing or saying something just to annoy you; it's just the way they see it. In any situation that you face, there will always be:

The way you see it – The way they see it – The way it is.

'Great Spirit, help me never to judge another until I have walked a mile in his moccasins.' – Sioux Indian saying

THERE IS A SOLUTION

You've purchased this book to find out how to manage difficult people, and that's what you *are* going to find out. It won't include beating them on the head with a baseball bat, putting poison in their tea or nailing them up in a crate and shipping them to Outer Mongolia. You will find out what to say and you'll develop the confidence to communicate your thoughts and needs.

This book will show you:

▓ How to deal with a difficult customer.

▓ How to manage difficult staff.

▓ What to say to a manipulative boss.

▓ How to handle any other Difficult Person you come into contact with.

However, we need to examine both sides of the interactions we have with other people. You need to consider what your role is in any interaction.

Are you a difficult person?

When I'm running a seminar on How To Manage Difficult People, I often say to the group:

> 'Please put up your hand if you're a difficult person who makes problems for other people.'

Guess what – not one person raises their hand! Now you're probably thinking that nobody is going to admit to this, particularly in public. But I believe that no one, in any way, regards themselves as a difficult person.

I've asked this question many times and, out of the hundreds of people who've attended this seminar, no one has put their hand up. They will, however, go on to tell me about all the difficult customers they have to deal with, their manipulative boss, their problem staff and the neighbours who won't keep their children under control.

These figures don't add up – we have hundreds of people who don't believe they are difficult, telling me about hundreds of people who are.

Why is it important

Research tells us that we spend 70–85% of our waking time interacting with other people. These interactions take place at work when we're:

- Dealing with customers or clients.

- Talking on the telephone.

- Negotiating.

- Managing people.

- Dealing with colleagues.

- Attending meetings.

- Interviewing.

- Conducting appraisals.

- Training.

In our personal life we interact with husbands, wives, partners, children, friends, family and neighbours. You'd need to live on a desert island or be a hermit in a cave to avoid communicating with other people. The Robinson Crusoes and the hermits of this world are few and far between. Most of us need, and want, to have interactions and relationships with other people. Do you remember how excited Robinson Crusoe was when he discovered a footprint in the sand and eventually met up with Man Friday? Human beings are social creatures and other people are by far the most important factors in our lives.

We allow, and you will note I say 'allow', these relationships with other people to decide how happy or unhappy we will be. Sad to say, many of these relationships are not good, be they in our personal or working lives. The problem is we just don't communicate well with each other.

I was recently talking with a guy at the gym who works for one of the major international banks. He was complaining about how he hated going to work in the morning, and that he only lived for the weekends and holidays. It turned out that he actually likes the job he does, and he feels well paid for it. However, his relationships with his colleagues were either poor or non-existent; he appeared to know lots of difficult people.

When I asked him what he was doing to resolve this situation, he said, 'Nothing'. He didn't believe that he could do anything about it.

Many of us can empathise with this situation – and we know it's not an isolated case. The question is: why does it happen? Why do we have problems with other people? I believe that too many people do not communicate well and find difficulty in expressing what they think and feel. Recent research suggests that 80% of people who fail at work do so because they cannot relate well to other people.

Most people do not communicate well because they haven't had the chance to learn good communication skills. What we are taught at school does not prepare us for the world in terms of communicating and relating with other uneducated people. Schools concentrate on our IQ and our ability to read, write, calculate and assimilate facts, figures and information. I don't remember being taught how to:

▓ Persuade an employer to give me a job.

▓ Really listen to people.

▓ Be assertive.

▓ Build rapport.

- Understand other people's behaviour.

- Motivate myself.

- Be more confident.

- Be more self-aware.

- Deal with people problems.

It's fair to say that many schools nowadays do address these issues, but they're fighting an uphill battle. Many children spend less time interacting with each other than was the case when I went to school. Children are delivered and uplifted from school by their parents. When they return home, they spend more time in their bedroom watching TV and using their computer. They have more Facebook friends than they have face-to-face friends. I spent time with my friends on the way to school and on the way home. When I did get home, I couldn't get out quick enough to play with my buddies. Of course, life was different then, but we're looking at our ability to get on with other people, and particularly the difficult ones.

As adults, we tend to fall back on any natural communication skills we may have, and pick things up as we go along. However, many people do not have natural interpersonal skills and learn very little as they go through life. We all experience this in terms of bad managers and salespeople, poor customer service and, sometimes, difficult relationships with colleagues and friends.

If we were to study any of the successful people in this world (and that means whatever success means to you) you will often find excellent communicators. These people are able to listen and understand, ask the right questions and react to all the non-verbal signals that each of us sends out. They are experts at selling themselves.

The most important thing to realise is that every day of our lives we are selling ourselves – nothing really happens until we're successful in doing that.

Your level of communication will determine how successful you will be with others: emotionally, personally and socially. It will also have a huge impact on your financial success. However, most importantly, your level of success in terms of your happiness, emotional wellbeing or anything else you desire is a direct result of how you communicate with yourself.

The most important relationship you'll ever have is the one you have with yourself.

IDENTIFYING DIFFICULT PEOPLE

Who do you regard as a 'difficult person'? It could be someone who bullies, manipulates and annoys you and causes you unhappiness and stress. They say or do things you don't like or find offensive and unacceptable. And, of course, this creates problems in the workplace.

According to research, 18.9 million working days every year are lost as a direct result of workplace bullying, costing the UK economy 6 billion pounds. This has a massive impact on productivity, creativity, morale and general employee wellbeing. At least one in four people will be bullied at some point during their working lives.

There is a whole range of behaviours that we could classify as difficult. How many of them drive you crazy?

Aggressive	Embarrassed
Angry	Forgetful
Antagonistic	Hostile
Anxious	Impatient
Apologetic	Impetuous
Argumentative	Indecisive
Biased	Insecure
Bigots	Insincere
Blamers	Intimidating
Bombastic	Intolerant
Boring	Late
Bossy	Liars
Bullies	Loners
Change resistant	Manipulators
Charmers	Messy
Cold	Miserable
Competitive	Moody
Complainers	Negative
Confrontational	Nit-pickers
Confused	Patronising
De-motivated	Phobic
Disobedient	Selfish

Shy	Unrealistic
Smarmy	Unsatisfied
Stressed	Weak
Timid	Workaholics
Unassertive	Vindictive
Unenthusiastic	Violent
Uninterested	Yes people

Wow! What a list, and you might want to add more. Take a look down the list and tick the behaviours that you would regard as difficult. Now, you may say 'all of them' but, when I do this exercise with participants in a seminar, they all have different views. Some individuals don't regard boring people as difficult, whereas they drive other people crazy! You may not give a hoot about unassertive people, but others would want to strangle them.

I'm an on-time person, and I always have a challenge with people who turn up late or don't keep to an agreed timescale. If someone says that they'll phone me back in an hour, that's what I expect them to do. They, on the other hand, may not have any real conception of time, and might phone me back in three hours. If my friends say, 'We'll meet in the pub at 8pm', I'll be there at 7.55pm. If you're an on-time person, then you'll empathise with this. If you're not, then you'll think I'm crazy, because to you it doesn't matter if someone shows up 10, 20 or 30 minutes late.

Let's look at some examples of difficult people and difficult situations.

The supervisor from hell

You've probably worked for a boss at some time in your life who gave you nothing but grief – you may still do. They don't necessarily reprimand or discipline you, but they make demands that you find difficult to fulfil.

I once had a sales supervisor called John who made my life hell. I learned so much from John, mainly how not to supervise people. I remember thinking at the time, 'When I become a manager or a supervisor, I will never treat anyone the way John treats me.' He demanded that I phone him every evening with details of how many customers I'd seen that day, how many demonstrations I'd done and how many orders I'd taken. As I rhymed off the numbers, he would come up with comments such as: 'How many?' 'Is that all?' 'Why was that?' 'Are you sure?' 'Why are you not as good as the other guys?' 'What are you going to do about it?' He inferred that if I didn't improve then I would probably lose my job.

The results I reported were never good enough and the successes were never recognised. I used to dread the evening telephone calls and I left home every morning with this huge pressure to perform better. Quite naturally, this didn't help me sell any better. He was really just a bully and he thought this was what management and supervision was all about. According to Professor Gary Cooper at The University of Manchester who has researched bullying in the workplace, 'You go from the psychopath who had a problem early in childhood who, when they get to a position of power, feel that if they make other people feel incompetent it must mean they are very competent themselves. These tend to be very insecure people.'

As you'd probably expect, I hated this job and spent most of my time plotting how to push John under a bus and how to get a new job. It also had the effect of seriously undermining my confidence. Although I'd been in sales for four years, I was starting to think that perhaps I wasn't good enough, and maybe it wasn't for me. If only I'd known then what I know now.

Ironically, when I did eventually find another job, John's boss, the National Sales Manager, asked me not to leave – he said I was one of their most promising salespeople.

The customer from hell

I'm also sure that sometime in your life you've experienced an unhappy customer or client. They berate you and seem to think that you are personally responsible for all the mistakes of your organisation.

I remember standing at the Virgin Atlantic check-in desk at Heathrow airport. There was a lady passenger at the next check-in desk screaming at the gentleman from Virgin, half in English and half in who knows what. The message obviously was that she was somewhat disappointed by the service she was receiving, would never fly with this airline again and that she'd probably like to kill somebody. The man from Virgin merely carried out his business trying to satisfy this customer, and probably thinking that he'd like to push her out of the aeroplane at 30,000 feet.

EasyJet in the UK and Southwest Airlines in the US both appear in fly-on-the-wall TV documentaries depicting the day-to-day running of their business. I've watched the easyJet programme several times, and it mainly features difficult customer situations. I cringe every time I hear an easyJet staff member speak to a difficult customer. They make life so much harder for themselves by their attitude, body language and choice of words. Of course, it makes good television, so there is no incentive to make any changes. They say that there's no such thing as bad publicity, but I often wonder how many new customers they might obtain by improving their approach.

The relationship from hell

The difficult person could be someone you live beside, a noisy neighbour or perhaps someone with disruptive children. It could also be someone in your own family and very close to you.

I was happily married for fourteen years and unhappily married for one. In that last year, it all went wrong. I totally believed at the time that it was my wife who was causing the problem. I won't bore you with all the gory details but it all boiled down to my belief that my wife's job was more important than me. It's a fairly classic case, and I look back now and realise I could have handled it a whole lot better. As I said earlier, 'I wish I'd known then what I know now.'

Whether it's a colleague, a customer or someone in your personal life, what it really comes down to is that the difficult person sees the world differently from you. There are people who deliberately want to make your life miserable, for reasons known only to themselves, but they are very much in the minority.

DO WE ALL HAVE THE SAME DIFFICULT PEOPLE?

I'm sure you've been in the situation where you describe a difficult person to a colleague or a friend and they don't appear to agree with you or understand what you're talking about.

A couple of years ago I had a call from Steve, a customer service manager working in the paper industry. He wanted me to run a seminar for his team on How to Manage Difficult Customers. I had several telephone conversations with Steve, organising dates, times and getting to understand his business. If I were to describe his style on the telephone I would use words such as businesslike, cold, curt and somewhat impatient. I started to realise that if I was one of his customers then I might have been a bit difficult. He certainly knew his business and I don't think he was a bad person, but warm and friendly – forget it.

On the day we ran the seminar, the group were discussing their customers, and one in particular that Steve thought was extremely difficult. He was going on about what a pain this customer was, always complaining and making demands. Amanda, one of the other participants, disagreed. She admitted that this particular customer was a bit of a challenge, but she got on all right with him. The other participants agreed with Amanda. Steve was incredulous; he couldn't understand how the members of his team couldn't see what a difficult person this customer was.

As you'll realise, Steve was making life tough for himself by his approach to customers. I'm not even sure how he came to be the manager!

'Your customers will get better when you do.' – Unknown author

There aren't that many about, honest!

Statistically, only about 2% of the population could be regarded as genuinely difficult, although I know that on some days you think you've come up against all of them! If you're having a problem with a difficult person, what you're really experiencing is *conflict*, which the dictionary defines as: 'A state of disharmony between incompatible or antithetical persons, ideas or interests; a clash'.

It will make life easier if you identify whether you are dealing with conflict or a genuinely difficult person. Truly difficult people are rare and you may have to accept that it isn't personal and they may just be that way. We'll come on to how you can deal with these people, but it might just be best to walk away. Conflict is personal and we may have to accept that we are part of the tension that is created. We will look at how to defuse that tension later in the book.

WHY ARE PEOPLE DIFFICULT?

As I said earlier, I find it hard to find anyone who admits to being difficult. But it's obvious that we've probably all been difficult for another person at some time in our life. And of course there's that 2% of the population who are genuinely difficult. So, what causes this difficulty?

▓ **Stress.** Some people get stressed for all sorts of reasons. Often it's just their inability to deal with aspects of their job and their personal life. They tend to blame other people and circumstances, but most often they have the answers within themselves.

▓ **Personal problems.** It's fair to say that people sometimes have problems that are outside of their control: a death in the family, breakdown of a marriage or a relationship, problems with children, or they may have health issues.

▓ **Not competent to do the job.** It's often the case in the workplace that people experience difficulty in doing their job and in finding help. Although they may not admit to this, they might feel inadequate and express their frustration by complaining, being negative and difficult.

▓ **Don't know they're being difficult.** Some people are not conscious of how they're perceived by others. They believe that their behaviour is quite normal and are unable to understand why some people see it otherwise.

▪ **They see the world differently.** We all see the world differently from each other. But some people's programming causes them to become annoyed when others don't see it as they see it.

▪ **Low self-esteem.** Some people's lack of self-confidence and belief in themselves often causes them to be angry at the world. They believe that other people are out to do them down and that everything is against them.

There is another key reason that makes some people appear to be difficult.

Lack of acknowledgement

If you are a manager or a team leader, do you find yourself getting frustrated by that difficult employee who never seems to do things quite right? The one who takes up so much of your time and attention? It's very easy to fall into the trap of condemning that person as a no-hoper or a 'problem child'. But have you ever considered why they might be behaving badly? It could be that they have a massive need for acknowledgement, either physical or psychological.

A human's need for acknowledgement is so strong that they'll sometimes behave badly to get that acknowledgement. I'm sure you're aware of children who behave badly in school just to get attention – well, adults do it too. Some years ago, before she died, I used to receive phone calls from my elderly mother telling me how unwell she was. When I would rush over the following day, I would find her hale and hearty and in good health – she just wanted acknowledgement from me.

Although vital to human beings, we all have a different need for acknowledgement, be it physical or psychological. Some of us are way down the scale, but others have a huge need for acknowledgement and demonstrate that in various ways. If you manage a team of people, then I'm sure there are some members of your team who demand more attention than others. When I was a field sales manager, I used to find that some of my salespeople phoned me much more than others. Often they were looking for help or reassurance; sometimes they just wanted to talk. Moreover, they just needed acknowledgement from me.

That person in your team who gives you all sorts of problems that are often difficult to understand may just be seeking acknowledgement. Withdrawing or failing to provide acknowledgement will cause people to become difficult.

Don't beat yourself up

Let's be clear about what we've covered. If you experience conflict and tension with another person, and someone else doesn't, that doesn't mean to say that you're necessarily in the wrong. You may say to yourself:

> 'That Mary in my office is a real pain – she makes things very difficult for me. Everyone else seems to think she's okay, so I must be wrong.'

If Mary is a difficult person for you, then accept it; you're entitled to feel as you do. You are not the same as the other people in your office. They may believe that Mary's behaviour is acceptable, but they see the world differently from you. Some people thought that Adolf Hitler was a nice guy, and I'm sure Osama Bin Laden had a lot of buddies who thought he was wonderful.

However (and I hear you saying, 'Here comes the big but!'), if you experience conflict and tension with another person, you have to change either the way you interact with them or the way they interact with you. You may decide not to interact with them at all, although that may not be possible if they're a colleague, a customer or a cantankerous old mother! I'm reminded at this moment of a quotation once credited to Abraham Lincoln (1809–65, 16th President of the United States):

'I don't think I like that man, I must get to know him better.'

CHANGING YOU OR CHANGING THEM?

It has to be said, you're not going to change them until you change you! Let's look at the *change you* bit. I'm not talking about changing your personality – I'm talking about making adjustments to your behaviour, which will make your life much easier. In order to do that, you need to:

▪ **Understand your own behaviour.** What is your dominant behaviour programme? Do you choose your behaviour or do other people choose it for you? Do you react or do you think?

- **Take charge of your behaviour.** Choose a behaviour programme to deal with any situation. Be aware of the results you expect from that behaviour.

- **Build your confidence and self-esteem.** You must believe in yourself before you can interact effectively with other people.

- **Improve your listening skills.** The effective communicator listens more than they speak.

- **Understand the impact of your tone of voice and your body language.** People are influenced more by how you say than what you say.

- **Become more assertive.** Submissive and aggressive behaviours are your built-in programmes; assertiveness needs to be learned.

- **Be likeable.** People are more likely to accept what you say if they like you. Nothing will happen until you sell yourself.

Later in the book we'll look at some techniques that can change or influence other people's behaviour towards you. But first, you need to have a better understanding of your own and other people's behaviour.

'Every moment that you spend upset, in despair, in anguish, angry or hurt because of the behaviour of anybody else in your life is a moment in which you have given up control of your life.'
– Dr Wayne Dyer (1940–, American psychotherapist, author, lecturer)

2

If You Don't Like the Programme – Change It!

FIRST IMPRESSIONS COUNT

A few years ago there was a television commercial for a major health insurance company. The strap line of this commercial was: 'You Are Amazing!' It made the point that every human being is unique and totally different from any other on the planet. People are such wonderful, complex and complicated individuals. Our bodies are all constructed differently, and our minds even more so!

When we meet and interact with other individuals we exchange all sorts of information. This is communicated by the words we use, our tone of voice and body language. Research by psychologists suggests that we all make about eleven decisions about other people within two minutes of meeting them. We decide whether we like the other person, what their background is, how intelligent they are, how positive or negative, how successful, and other factors that are important to us as individuals. We tend to stick with these decisions until proved otherwise.

I read a report in the media just before the Wimbledon tennis tournament in 2008. It was suggesting that many people didn't want Andy Murray, the Scottish tennis player, to do well in the tournament. These people said that they didn't like him, based on seeing him interviewed on TV or playing tennis. They felt he was too dour and lacked personality. Some people even suggested that he would be a difficult person to deal with.

This fast decision-making process, based on very little information, be it right or wrong, is one of our built-in programmes. When our cavemen ancestors were wandering around, club in hand, in a hostile environment, they often came upon other cavemen and scary creatures. In order to survive, they had to make quick decisions – 'Do I strike up a conversation with this other creature, do I make a run for it or do I bash them with my club?' It was also difficult for them in those days, because they didn't have mirrors and often didn't realise that the creature they encountered was no more hairy and ugly than they were themselves.

So be very much aware that, when someone meets you for the first time or speaks to you on the phone, they are making several decisions about you, just as you are making decisions about them. They may even be deciding within seconds if you're a difficult person and, of course, you may also come to the same decision. At this point, you may be saying to yourself, 'That's just too bad, because I am as I am. I was born this way, I was brought up this way and there's not much I can do about it.' Well, there is, so bear with me.

I remember once running a customer service workshop for some Telecom engineers. One of the participants, let's call him Colin, said very little for the whole two days he was there. He mostly glowered at me and looked thoroughly unpleasant. I thought to myself, 'That guy Colin hates me – he looks really aggressive. He looks like he'd like to beat me up! He's obviously taking nothing from this workshop.' When we'd finished at the end of the second day, Colin approached me as everyone was clearing up: 'Alan, I'd just like to say that I thoroughly enjoyed this workshop, I learned a lot and you were very considerate to me. I don't normally say very much, but you didn't put me under any pressure and I felt very relaxed.' You could have knocked me down with a feather. This was the last thing I expected from Colin and, after speaking to him for a few minutes and getting to know him, I reckoned he was a decent guy. But the message he was sending out to me was totally the opposite.

So, are we stuck with our behaviours? Can we do anything about it and do we want to?

CHANGING YOUR BEHAVIOUR

Remember what I said at the end of Chapter 1. We are not talking about personality; we are talking about behaviour and you can change your behaviour much easier than your personality.

Psychologists will argue as to the level of personality traits we are born with. I believe that we have certain personality tendencies and that our parents nurture these tendencies. For example, parents may recognise that they have a shy child. They may say to other people: 'He is really shy, he doesn't talk much and he's nervous of people.' The child hears and picks up on this, and behaves just as his parents have described.

I once sat down to Christmas dinner with family members, some of which were young children. Not mine, I hasten to add. At one point I offered vegetables to one of the children, but, before he could accept or reject them, his grandmother jumped in with: 'He doesn't like vegetables and he never eats them.' If this child hears this all the time, he never will eat vegetables. Like most children, I didn't particularly like vegetables when I was young. Nevertheless, my mother made it perfectly clear to my brother and I that you did eat your vegetables. It wasn't a choice; it was just what you did. It's like learning to cross the road. Children don't want to look right and left and right again. Your parents programme this into your subconscious in order to ensure your survival. By insisting on vegetable eating, my mother was looking after my colon's survival.

I believe that no matter what personality traits you were born with, whether introverted or extroverted, you can make changes to your behaviour whatever your age.

I was regarded as a fairly shy child and felt the consequences of this throughout my adolescence. Yes, there were girlfriends, but often they had to do most of the running due to my shyness and insecurities. At age 19, I was serving an engineering apprenticeship in a Glasgow factory. I developed a huge crush on one of the girls who worked in the Drawing Office. She was dark and slim, and I fell for her bubbly personality. But how could she have possibly been interested in me and, after all, I was too shy to find out. After some goading from a few of my friends, I plucked up the courage and, with my heart thumping in my chest, I made the phone call: 'Would you like to go to a party on Saturday?' was my nervous question. 'I would really love to and thank you for asking' was the response that sent my little heart soaring!

The lesson I learned from all of this was that, although you may have a shy personality, you can make small changes to your behaviour to get what you want.

We are not born self-conscious or full of self-doubt. We are not born unhappy, jealous, ashamed, angry, competitive or difficult. We are born confident, carefree, curious about everything, happy, fearless and full of energy.

Use your personal supercomputer

The human brain is a fantastic piece of equipment and it is often compared with electro-mechanical systems and computers. However, when you look at the facts, these comparisons are almost meaningless. For example, if you compare all the telephone systems that are currently operating in the world today, their sum total in comparison to your brain would occupy a part the size of a baked bean. When compared to the world's supercomputers, the brain is so far advanced it is unbelievable. One supercomputer working at a hundred million calculations per second would have to operate for 100 years to accomplish what your brain can do in a minute.

Research has established that the brain is made up of millions of cells called neurons. There are probably about 10 billion neurons in the average human brain. These work by passing tiny amounts of electricity from one to another. These neural activities control muscles and all the activities of the body. It is often thought that the brain's ability to perform declines with age. How many times have you heard a middle-aged or older person say, 'I'm too old to learn anything, my memory is failing, I am no longer creative'? This attitude is summarised in the saying: 'You can't teach an old dog new tricks'. But you can!

The good news is that the brain does not deteriorate as we once thought. Research conducted by Professor Mark Rosenzweig established that, if the brain is stimulated at any age, it will grow more cells. So, although some cells may die with age, it is possible to grow new ones. I am sure you must be aware or have heard of people who, well into their seventies and eighties, are still performing well mentally. There are people who learn languages in later life, who complete university degrees, who learn to play a musical instrument. These are the people who take charge of their thinking, who stimulate the brain into action. If we lost 10,000 brain cells from the day we were born until we were 90, we would probably only have lost about 2% of our capacity.

Some researchers into the brain believe that everything we have ever seen, heard or experienced is recorded in our brain. I find this difficult to comprehend; however, I have remembered situations in dreams that I would have great difficulty in recalling while awake. I have dreamt situations from my childhood that I would have thought were totally lost to me. The brain is an amazing piece of equipment and people who have studied it still know very little. I'm always intrigued when computer experts find difficulty in identifying a fault or establishing why it did whatever it did. After all, humans built the computer – shouldn't we understand it? We will never really understand the workings of the brain when we consider how superior it is to any computer.

> *'One machine can do the work of 50 ordinary men. No machine can do the work of one extraordinary man.'* – Elbert Hubbard
> (1859–1915, American author and publisher)

The human brain is extremely complex but, to aid our understanding of behaviour and how we can use that to manage difficult people, I've divided it up into six programmes.

USING THE SIX PROGRAMMES OF BEHAVIOUR

When you're managing difficult people it's helpful to understand that each of us communicates from a particular behaviour programme. Each programme has both negative and positive aspects. No matter what your personality is, you can choose the behaviour you want to create positive experiences for the people you interact with. As I describe the following programmes, you'll see how your behaviour can influence the behaviour of other people.

The six programmes

- The fun programme

- The passive programme

- The defiant programme

- The controlling programme

- The caring programme

- The thinking programme

You can use your supercomputer brain to select any one of these programmes, at any time to suit your needs. You do, however, have a default programme, and I'll explain more about that later.

Let's examine the characteristics of each of these behaviour programmes and we'll look at the positive and negative consequences of each.

The fun programme

This programme contains the feelings you were born with – it's the part of you that is natural and impulsive. Your fun programme, as it states, is about having fun, laughing and making other people laugh. It's about playing games, going to a party and generally enjoying yourself. Your fun programme could light up a difficult conversation and make the other person feel at ease.

However, on the negative side, this would not be a good idea if the other person is a bit serious and making fun could make the situation worse. It makes sense to say that you wouldn't choose your fun programme if you were attending a funeral or any other event where quiet and subdued behaviour is more appropriate.

The passive programme

This programme includes feelings that you've learned such as guilt, depression and some of your fears. Children, for example, are born with two fears – loud noises and falling – they learn everything else. Fear of flying or fear of dogs is something you learn. You often find that, if a parent has a fear of dogs, then the child learns that fear.

Using your passive programme could sometimes be positive such as when you're willing to give up your point of view and compromise in order to resolve a situation. It's about fitting in and adapting to circumstances. It can be useful when you need to give way to a difficult person.

On the negative side, the passive programme can be used in a manipulative way. A difficult person would use it to get what they want from somebody else. Someone who's communicating out of their passive programme might display victim behaviour, act pitiful and make 'poor me' statements. You then feel obliged to make them happy by whatever means. A person in their passive programme may whine a lot and look for someone else to take responsibility for a situation.

If you're communicating out of your passive programme, then this could be very stressful for you – always having to give way to the other person is not very productive.

The defiant programme

This is the programme where all your angry behaviour comes from. It leads to statements such as: 'There's no way you're getting away with this!' or 'Just you try and stop me!' It's very physical, threatening, loud and angry behaviour. When someone is in their defiant programme, it can make them hard to handle, particularly when a compromise is needed.

On the positive side, the defiant programme offers strength, courage and determination.

The controlling programme

This programme comes from your value system and is dependent on how you were brought up, your family and your culture. It is very much about the rules by which you live your life and judge how other people should behave.

The controlling programme knows all the answers and has opinions on everything; it is critical and judgemental. As a result, it makes many demands on other people, tells people what to do and tries to manipulate them. This programme knows all the rules – the have tos, the ought tos and the shoulds. When a person's controlling programme is aware of someone not doing things correctly, they take satisfaction in telling that person how to do it right. Prejudice also comes from your controlling programme.

On the positive side, your controlling programme contains all the skills you've learned. These are the things that you do in a fairly automatic way, such as getting dressed, driving a car and cooking a meal. You give hardly a thought to these actions, although they may have been difficult when you first learned them. The controlling programme runs things very efficiently and handles emergency situations with confidence.

The caring programme

This programme is about being sympathetic and helpful. It's about taking care of other people and also taking care of you. It is your caring programme that looks after other people and shows willingness to help them when they are in a difficult situation. When you see someone who is in pain or suffering in some way and you offer to help, you're acting out of your caring programme. When you look after yourself by exercising or by being aware of your diet, you're acting from this programme.

On the negative side, the caring programme can create problems when it interferes and tries to help when the other person doesn't want to be helped.

The thinking programme

This programme gathers information, analyses data and situations. It develops options and makes decisions. When you communicate out of your thinking programme, you appear cool, calm and collected. You communicate rationally, logically and reasonably. This programme is based on facts not emotions. It is about thinking and not reacting. This is different to other programmes, such as controlling and caring, where we may react to situations based on our rules and beliefs. Neither is it about reacting to our feelings as we may do from our fun, passive and defiant programmes.

This is the best programme to communicate from when you are dealing with difficult people, particularly when they are in their defiant or controlling programmes. Communicating from your thinking programme is more likely to cause the difficult person to act out of their thinking programme also.

Now that you have a better understanding of each behaviour programme, let's try a little test. The following statements come from a particular behaviour programme. Write beside each statement, or on a separate piece of paper, whether it is from the fun, passive, defiant, controlling, caring or thinking programme.

'Wow, that's fantastic!'

'I'm really fed up!'

'How dare he talk to me like that!'

'You don't look too good, are you feeling okay?'

'He shouldn't be saying things like that.'

'Let's see what information I need to take care of this situation.'

You should have:

Fun

Passive

Defiant

Caring

Controlling

Thinking

Don't worry too much if you have something different as you may hear these words in your head in a particular way. You are reading these statements, whereas the tone of voice in which they're said also influences which behaviour programme they come from. I've said that 'How dare he talk to me like that!' is from the defiant programme because I hear it as really angry and emotional. If the person was less emotional and more controlled, it would come across as the controlling programme. However, it's unlikely that 'Wow, that's fantastic!' could ever be anything other than the fun programme.

INVITING PROGRAMMES

Let's look at how the different behaviour programmes affect other people. When someone is acting out of a particular behaviour programme, it invites a programme from the other person. For example, if you were talking with someone and they were acting from their defiant programme, they might use words such as:

> 'There is no way I'm paying you that money. You can go and
> get lost, and if you come around here to collect it you'll get a
> punch in the mouth!'

What programme do you think the other person would use to respond to this? What would they say? Put yourself in that person's shoes.

It's unlikely you'd switch on the fun programme. Making a joke or trying to get a laugh in some way would not be the best thing to do. If the other person is displaying totally defiant behaviour and you respond from your fun programme, then you are liable to get punched.

I don't think you'd use the caring programme, saying something like:

> 'You poor dear, are you a bit upset? Why don't you have a nice
> cup of tea?'

That could also put you on the receiving end of some physical violence. What is most likely to happen is that you will resort to the fight or flight response. You may fight by reacting from your defiant programme and respond with something like:

> 'You just try and punch me in the mouth and see what
> happens. You'll get it right back!'

You may switch on your controlling programme and say:

'Please do not talk to me in that manner – that is no way to talk to someone. If you continue, I will be forced to cut off this conversation.'

What tends to happen, particularly with a member of staff dealing with a customer in the defiant programme, is that the member of staff slips into the passive programme, saying something like:

'I'm terribly sorry – perhaps we've made a mistake with your account. I've not been involved in this. I'll need to speak to my supervisor.'

It is also possible that you'll switch on your thinking programme, but let's come back to that.

Look at the list below and write beside each programme, or on a separate piece of paper, the programme the other person might use to respond to you.

Programme used   Programme used to respond

Fun

Passive

Defiant

Caring

Controlling

Thinking

How did you get on? This is what you should have:

Fun

Controlling

Defiant, controlling or passive

Passive

Controlling or passive

Thinking

Fun invites fun

If someone is in the fun programme, it normally invites the fun programme from the other person. If you meet with friends and you say:

'Great to see you, let's go for a drink and have a few laughs!'

they're most likely to respond from their fun programme with:

'Hey, that's a great idea, I feel like a few laughs!'

However, as I said earlier, if you were to approach someone in your fun programme and they were either depressed or angry, then you would probably invite another behaviour programme:

> 'It's all right for you laughing and joking but I don't feel well
> and you are making me worse.'

A person in the defiant or controlling programme may say to someone in their fun programme:

> 'Why don't you shut up, you stupid fool, and get lost!'

Passive invites controlling

Sometimes the 'poor me' passive person invites the caring programme. You could hear conversations such as:

> 'I'm really fed up. These customers are always finding fault and
> I'm doing my best, but it never seems good enough.'

The other person, using their caring programme, may say:

> 'Poor old you. Why don't I make you a nice cup of tea and I'm
> sure you'll feel better.'

Nonetheless, if someone is in the passive programme, then, sad to say, the other person is more likely to respond with controlling. Passive, non-assertive people tend to be linked with and invite controlling people.

Defiant invites passive

It is possible that a person in defiant programme could invite defiant from the other person:

'If you speak to me like that again, I'll throw you out that door!'

Or it may invite the controlling programme:

'That is no way to speak to me. If you continue, I will close your account.'

The defiant programme is most likely to invite the passive programme:

'I'm really sorry, I do apologise. I'll do everything I can to help you.'

Caring invites passive

The caring programme tends to invite the passive programme from the other person. The caring person may say:

'You're not looking too well. Are you feeling okay? Do you want me to phone a doctor?'

The other person responding from the passive programme would say:

'I'm feeling a bit sick. I think I'll be okay if I lie down for a while.'

Controlling invites passive

A person communicating from their controlling programme could invite controlling back. If the controlling person were to say something like:

> 'I want this car fixed today – I'm not prepared to wait any longer. You people need to take a long hard look at yourselves and improve your customer service.'

The other person, replying from their controlling programme, may say:

> 'We will have your car fixed just as soon as we get round to it. We repair hundreds of cars and we are not about to give you priority.'

That same person may also reply in their defiant programme, becoming very angry and saying:

> 'Don't you tell me to improve our customer service. You're not my boss and I don't need people like you telling me what to do!'

What is most likely to happen is that this person responds from their passive programme:

> 'I'm really sorry your car is not ready. We had to wait for new parts to be delivered, and then the mechanic working on your car got sick and had to go home.'

Thinking invites thinking

The thinking programme will nearly always invite the thinking programme back from the other person. If you're dealing with a difficult person in their defiant or controlling programme, then you won't change their behaviour initially. But if you continue to use your thinking programme then *they* are much more likely to change to their thinking programme and become more reasonable.

If a difficult customer was in their controlling programme, saying:

'I want that car fixed today.'

the thinking programme would say:

'I understand that you're angry and annoyed, Mr Smith. If my car wasn't ready, I'd probably feel the same way. We are unable to fix your car today due to the fact that the new parts have not arrived. We have sent our van round to the parts depot, instead of waiting for them to deliver, and we will have your car up and running by 12 noon tomorrow. If it helps we will have it delivered to your door.'

All of this is delivered in a calm, confident, friendly and professional voice. The body language is open and the words used are 'thinking words', which I'll explain later.

MAKING THE RIGHT CHOICE

The thinking programme is not always the most natural for people. We tend to respond based on our emotions. Human beings are primarily driven by their emotions and our flight or fight response. When we interact with a difficult person, we resort to the passive programme (flight):

'Why is he getting on to me? It's not my fault.'

Or the defiant programme (fight):

'Don't you dare speak to me like that. There's no way I'm taking that from you!'

Or the controlling programme (fight):

'People like you always behave this way. I'm not going to listen to a word you say.'

When I ask people in a seminar if they have a choice as to which behaviour they choose, many people initially say 'no'. They say things such as:

'If someone treats me badly or speaks to me in a nasty way, I let them know about it!'

'Some people really make me mad!'

'Some customers really get me down and stress me out.'

I then ask the seminar participants to tell me: 'Who owns your body? Who owns your brain? Who owns your behaviour?' The majority of participants realise or come to accept that they are in charge of their behaviour – that they do have a choice as to how they communicate with other people. It's often difficult but, once the skills are learned, it makes life so much easier for us all.

'You are either part of the solution or part of the problem.' – Eldridge Cleaver (1935–98, African American leader, writer)

SELF-FULFILLING PROPHECY

Has this ever happened to you? You're about to meet or speak to a customer, a new colleague or even somebody in your social life, and someone else describes this person to you. Let me give you an example of what I mean.

I was running a seminar at a client's office and I was discussing the arrangements for getting into the building and finding the training room with my contact, Steve. He explained that I had to check in with the security guard at the reception desk. 'You'll not get much help from him,' says Steve. 'He's a typical security guard, a grumpy old so 'n' so and he won't be much help.' My first response, when I arrived at the office, was to prepare to do battle with this typical security guard. However, at the last moment I checked myself and decided to practise what I preach. I approached the security guard, told him who I was in a warm and friendly manner, and asked for directions to the training room. John, as his name badge indicated, said that he'd need to make a few phone calls to find out where my room was. In between these calls, we exchanged some small talk, and even managed some comments about the local football team's performance the night before.

Initially John was a bit grumpy but after a while he warmed up and, ultimately, couldn't have been more helpful. I treated him with respect, I spent time getting to know him and I expected him to respond in a helpful manner – and that's how he responded. Steve, of course, had this thing in his head about typical security guards and treated John accordingly. He expected John to be grumpy and unhelpful – so that was how John responded to him.

People will often respond just as you expect; it's a self-fulfilling prophecy. So, if you're about to meet someone new, do not let other people decide your behaviour. You have to decide who runs your mind. Is it you or is it somebody else?

DECIDING YOUR DEFAULT PROGRAMME

We tend to switch between the different programmes but most of us have a dominant or default programme. This is the programme that we resort to most of the time.

Let's look at each of the programmes again and think of some personalities, sports people or politicians who are dominant in each of the programmes. I'm sure you'll have your own ideas, but here are some of mine.

▓ **Fun.** You could probably name almost any comedian or funny person on TV. My choice would be Chandler Bing, one of the characters in the TV programme *Friends*. He always has a funny remark to make, and it sometimes gets him into trouble.

▓ **Passive.** Sticking with the *Friends* theme, how about Ross Geller in this programme. He always seems to be whining and having things happen to him. In some situations he seems like a nice guy but, after a while, he can be a bit annoying.

▓ **Defiant.** Supermodel Naomi Campbell pops into mind. She has had more than her share of publicity over her inability to keep her temper. I believe one judge in court ordered her to attend an anger management programme.

▓ **Caring.** Although no longer with us, Princess Diana was always regarded as a caring person – this seemed to be her default programme.

▓ **Controlling.** Margaret Thatcher, the ex-Prime Minister of the UK, was a classic controlling person. She always knew what was best for the country and made sure that everyone was aware of her views.

▓ **Thinking.** I believe that President Obama communicates from his thinking programme. He appears to listen, gather information and make a reasonable decision.

You might disagree with me in some or all of these, but I hope you realise where I'm coming from. It may also help you consider what your default programme of behaviour is. Let me give you an example of my programmes of behaviour. At the time of writing this, I've just had an incident with one of my teeth. A few months ago, I had two crowns fitted and last night, while I was flossing, one of them fell out. I went off to bed in passive programme: 'Why does this happen to me? This cost me a lot of money and it'll now cost more. I've also got to go through all the stuff in the dentist's chair.' I was having a right old whinge to myself. Then my defiant programme kicked in: 'I'm not having this, it's a disgrace, spending all that money and it still isn't right. I'll be letting that dentist know all about it!' I then realised that I would never get to sleep in this emotional state, so I switched on the thinking programme: 'Tomorrow I will phone the dentist and make an appointment. I'm sure it won't take long to get it sorted and I can ask him to look at another tooth I've been concerned about.' I then fell asleep.

Our passive, controlling and defiant programmes can be very stressful for us and obviously unhealthy. Using your thinking programme is so much better for your health and welfare, and also for getting the job done. Thinking is very rarely a person's default programme – it needs to learned and developed. It is absolutely vital when faced with a difficult person so let's take a closer look in the next chapter.

3

Build a Better Frame of Mind

USING THE FIVE FACTORS OF SUCCESS

If you want to be an expert in managing difficult people, you need to develop physical and psychological fitness. People who are consistently successful in dealing with difficult people demonstrate five essential characteristics. I like to call them the Five Factors of Success:

- Mind control

- Belief

- Energy

- Rapport

- Courage

Developing these five factors will not only ensure your success in managing difficult people, it will also contribute to your success in life.

1 MIND CONTROL

Before we can achieve anything in our life, we need to take charge of our thinking. Take charge of your thinking and you take charge of your life.

Thinking is about all those little conversations that go on in your mind – all the thousands of things you say to yourself every minute of your waking day. Someone once worked out that we have around 12,367 thoughts every day, and about 70% of these are negative.

I had a very sombre voice mail message from my accountant the other day. He said: 'Alan, I need you to phone me about your tax situation.' I, of course, like any other normal person, immediately thought the worst and believed it was going to cost me money. It turned out that the tax office owed me money and I received a nice little rebate. But for a short while I did feel a bit low and apprehensive.

Your thoughts control your emotions and as a result how you act. Every invention in the world began as thought. Thoughts are so powerful. If you think positive thoughts, you'll get positive results: happiness, prosperity, heath and loving relationships. Think negative thoughts and you'll get negative results: stress, sickness and unhappiness.

'We are what we think. All that we are arises with our thoughts. With our thoughts, we make our world.' – Buddha (568–488 BC, founder of Buddhism)

Negative thoughts are too expensive

Thinking and talking negatively to yourself or to anyone else is going to cost you a great deal in terms of stress, loss of self-esteem, broken relationships. It will also prevent you getting what you want out of life.

Do you ever catch yourself saying any of these?

'It's going to be one of those days.'

'I'm tired.'

'I'm fed up.'

'I can't seem to get things right.'

'I'm losing patience.'

'I'm no good at this.'

'Why doesn't anything go right for me?'

'I'm always late.'

'With my luck I don't stand a chance.'

'I'm really unfit.'

'If only I could win the lottery.'

'If I win the lottery it would give me lots of problems.'

It's estimated that 77% of the things we say to ourselves are negative, counterproductive and self-defeating. We're holding ourselves back. The problem is that these thoughts that we have in our conscious mind add to or confirm the programmes that are already in our subconscious.

If you drop something and say:

'I'm so clumsy!'

your subconscious mind receives the message and in effect says:

'Okay, you're clumsy – I'll give lots of clumsy.'

People about to speak in front of a group sometimes say to themselves:

'I'll probably get stuck for words and freeze up.'

Their subconscious minds absorb this and take action. What happens? They freeze up.

When we find ourselves having to manage a difficult person we might think:

'This person is going to give me a real problem. They'll probably moan and complain, and I won't be able to do anything about it.'

If this is the way you think, then that's probably what will happen. The subconscious mind believes what you tell it if you say it often enough and strongly enough. Negative self-talk is too expensive! It will cost you dearly if you allow it to continue.

I'm always fascinated by the people who lift huge weights, particularly in competitions like the Olympic Games. There are events for men and women and they get up on stage to lift a bar with huge weights attached. I often wonder what sort of things they're saying to themselves as they pace up and down, rubbing their hands with resin powder and taking huge breaths. What if they were saying:

> 'That looks really heavy – it's heavier than anything I've lifted before. I'll probably drop it, make a real fool of myself and even injure myself to boot . . . !'

What's going to happen if they say all this stuff to themselves? Their subconscious will say:

> 'Okay, you say you're going to drop it. Then that's what I'll arrange, and I'll try to make sure you injure yourself at the same time.'

Of course, that isn't what happens. This weight lifter, who's trained for years to do precisely this thing, is screaming at him- or herself internally:

> 'You're going to lift that bar and push it right through the ceiling! You're going to break the world record! You're going to win this competition and everyone in the world will see you doing it!'

In the day-to-day tasks that we face in our life, we should be no different from these sportsmen and women. Think negative thoughts and that's what your subconscious will focus upon. If you think illness, you'll become ill. If you think gloom and doom, that's what you'll get. But if you think health, happiness and success, you're already there.

> *'Most people are as happy as they make up their minds to be.'* –
> Abraham Lincoln

I read this quote some years ago and I know some people have a problem with it. We all face difficult situations in our lives and some people more than others. However, I've made up my mind to be as happy as I can and I recommend you do the same.

Focus on the positive things in your life – the things you can do, not the things you can't. Think about what you have achieved in the past, not what you haven't. Look at where you are going, not where you have been.

Focus on the positive

There's a story about a young man who was really into positive thinking. His workmates used to make a fool of him and, of course, he was challenged by their taunts. He told them one day that positive self-talk was so powerful that, if he told himself he could fly through the air, he'd be able to fly. 'Prove it,' they cried. So off he went, up to the twentieth floor of the building that they worked in. He jumped off and was heard to cry as he went past a tenth-floor window: 'Well, it's all going great so far.'

That sort of thinking isn't what this book is about. I sometimes get tired of hearing people say, 'Think positive.' What I'm suggesting is that in all the things we face in life we focus on the positive aspects.

Say, for example, a customer complains to you about some aspect of your product or service. It's so easy to think: 'We've messed up. We're going to lose this customer's business. This is a disaster!' It's far better to think: 'Okay, we've made a mistake. What can we learn from this so that we don't do it again and make our service even better?'

Ironically, it's often the case that, if you solve a customer's problem, apologise and recover well, the customer will forgive you and become even more loyal.

Here's another example of what I mean. Say you were to discover a small lump in some part of your body or a mark on your skin. Positive thinking might cause you to say:

'It's nothing. I'll leave it and it'll go away by itself.'

Negative thinking, on the other hand, would have you say:

'Oh no! I've got cancer. I'm going to be in pain and misery and I might die.'

Focusing on the positive allows you to say:

'I must get this looked at immediately, whatever it is. They have marvellous ways of removing and curing these things nowadays.'

There will always be challenges to face with customers and the people who work for you. Focusing on the positive will make them so much easier to deal with.

Be aware of what you say to yourself

For the next two days I want you to listen to the self-talk that goes on in your mind and what you say to other people and ask yourself:

'Is what I'm saying now allowing me to be confident, on top and going for it?'

If so, then great! Or:

'Is it holding me back and stopping me achieving what I want out of life?'

If this is the case, *Stop it – change the programme!*

Like many people, I've followed the career of Richard Branson and his Virgin Empire. Several years ago I read that Branson, who at the time had a string of successful record stores, was going to start an airline. I can recall some people saying:

'Who does Richard Branson think he is? How can he start up an airline and compete with the other large, existing and powerful carriers in the world? It's a massive task and, let's face it, aeroplanes cost an enormous amount of money in addition to whatever else you need to back up a flying operation.'

Branson, however, had no self-doubts – or at least none that he allowed to hold him back. He started by leasing a single aircraft – the rest, as they say, is history. Richard Branson has positive self-belief, which gives him positive expectations, causing positive decisive behaviour. It's available to all of us; we just have to focus on the positive.

Think, don't react

How you think – your relationship with yourself – is what's going to decide how well you communicate and deal with difficult people. The most important relationship you'll ever have is the one you have with yourself, so you've got to get that right. Henry Ford (1863–1947, American industrialist, founder of the Ford Motor Company), the guy who started all the traffic chaos, said:

> *'Thinking is the hardest work there is; that's why so few people do it.'*

People who are successful at managing difficult people have a deep understanding of their own minds. They're aware of their needs, their strengths and weaknesses, and their emotions. They're honest with themselves and, as a result, with the people they interact with.

Successful people have confidence in themselves; they accept their weaknesses but they don't see them as failure. They speak out when they don't know something and they ask for help when they need it.

Have you ever asked a question at a meeting possibly feeling a bit stupid and thinking everyone else knows the answer? At the coffee break someone then says:

'I'm glad you asked that question because I didn't know either but I didn't like to ask.'

Successful people have the courage to challenge what they hear in their own mind and also what they hear from other people.

2 BELIEF

The second of the five factors is Belief. It's very dependent on how we control our mind and the conversations we have with ourselves. Belief in yourself is what drives your motivation and that in turn generates the energy to manage a difficult person. A person who doesn't have belief in themselves or in what they're doing is going to find life very difficult. Of course it can be challenging to retain belief in yourself when you're under pressure from your customers, your boss or anyone else in your life.

I started planning my Speaking and Training business in 1993. At the time many well-meaning people would say things like:

'You're very brave – the training business is very competitive.'

'Do you think this is the best time to start a business?'

'Where are you going to find any clients that don't already have a training provider?'

If I had taken all this on board, my business would never have left the ground. But I believed I could do it. Of course I had my moments of doubt, but these were all reactions not thinking.

It was the same when I wrote my first book and, if you've ever been through this process, you'll know what I mean: rejection, rejection, rejection. I sent my book proposal to lots of publishers in the US, UK, Australia and Singapore. I received lots of charming letters, more or less saying that they didn't think they could sell this book. In order to reinforce my belief in myself, I kept thinking about people like J.K. Rowling, the *Harry Potter* author who was rejected dozens of times. I believe the people who wrote the first *Chicken Soup* book had to self-publish as no publisher would take them on.

I said earlier that it's tough to hold onto belief in yourself when other people in your life are telling you all the things you can't do. You must get that positive self-talk going, focus on the positive and believe in yourself.

Forget about goals

Many motivational speakers and self-help books will tell you that you must have goals. I've even advocated goal setting myself in the past. You write down your goals and detail them for family life, friends, finances, career, recreation, health, learning, education and your spiritual life. However, I've now come to the conclusion that successful people with strong self-belief don't do goal setting in this way. Why? Because they're too busy doing what they need to do to get what they want to get.

Successful people don't spend time writing down what they want out of life – they just get on and do it. To be successful at whatever it is we want to do, we need to ask ourselves:

'What do I really want to achieve?'

'What are my dreams and desires?'

'What do I want to build, to create?'

'What sort of person do I want to be?'

You need to clearly identify what it is you want out of life. What do you hunger and thirst for? What do you really want to accomplish?

If someone held your head under water you'd quickly realise what you wanted – oxygen! You need to feel like this to be successful. Most of us experience this feeling when we fall in love. We do almost anything to impress and be with the person of our dreams.

This is how people create success, it's how new countries were discovered, products were invented, Everest was conquered and man walked on the moon. You may not want to achieve something so dramatic – you may want to have a successful plumbing business or be an excellent accountant, run a marathon or just be able to manage the difficult people in your life. Whatever it is, once you identify and focus on it you will release the motivation to make it happen.

Know where you want to go

There is an often-told story of the swimmer Florence Chadwick. On her first attempt to swim the English Channel she encountered huge waves and chilling temperature. Her trainers were alongside her in a boat. They had greased her body to provide protection from the cold and gave her hot soup from a vacuum flask. She had everything going for her to ensure she was successful.

However, a heavy fog set in and as the fog descended her vision was limited to only a few feet. The water seemed to get colder, the waves higher and she started suffering from cramp in her arms and legs. She eventually gave up her effort and asked her trainers to take her on board the boat. What she didn't realise was that she was only a short distance from the shore. When the reporters asked her why she'd given up when she had just a short distance to go, her answer was quite simple:

> 'I lost sight of my goal. I'm not sure that I had it firmly in my mind.'

You need to have a clear mental picture of where you want to go. You need to visualise yourself being successful and work towards it. You then have a far better chance of achieving what you want to achieve.

And in case you're wondering about Florence Chadwick, she did become the first woman to swim the English Channel on 8 August 1950. It took her 13 hours and 25 minutes, and I bet her arms were tired!

Get out of your comfort zone

Think about what you're doing each day and ask yourself: 'Is what I'm doing now getting me to where I want to get to?' If the answer is 'No', then do something different. Get out of your comfort zone and change your habits.

An instructor was watching me use a piece of equipment in the gym the other day. 'Let me show you a different way to do it,' says he. As you'll guess, the different way was a lot harder, somewhat more painful and a lot more likely to produce results.

The human body will always find an easy way to do things and so does your brain. However, as we all know, no pain – no gain. So, if you want something different to happen, do something different.

The American psychologist Abraham Maslow (1908–70) said:

> *'If you deliberately plan to be less than you are capable of being, then I warn you that you will be unhappy for the rest of your life. You will be evading your own capabilities, your own possibilities.'*

Remember what I said earlier about the negative things we say to ourselves and the beliefs we have about ourselves – don't allow them to hold you back.

Change your beliefs

If you do have negative beliefs about yourself, here's a way to change them. Your subconscious will always attempt to move away from pain and towards pleasure. So start to associate massive pain to your negative belief. Think about how it will hold you back and stop you achieving what you're trying to achieve. Think about how miserable you'll feel if you don't even try.

Old people rarely regret what they've done in their life but they do regret what they haven't done. So think forward to when you're 75 or 80 years of age and imagine how you'll feel if you've never tried. Then start to think of the pleasure you'll receive in fulfilling your beliefs. Think about how good you'll feel when you achieve what you set out to do. If when you're older you look back and think about things you didn't achieve, at least you'll be able to say: 'I tried, I gave it my best shot and I didn't sit on the sidelines.'

3 ENERGY

If you are going to be successful in managing difficult people, then you need lots of energy. You need brain energy and you need body energy.

Brain energy

Managing difficult people puts huge demands on your levels of brain energy. I'm sure you come away from a difficult interaction with someone, perhaps a customer or your boss, feeling totally drained and perhaps a bit shaky. That's because your metabolism has been working flat out. It's what is better known as stress!

When you get stressed, a whole cocktail of chemicals rushes through your system. Again, it's the fight or flight response. Our adrenal system releases hormones and adrenaline to help you fight or run away. When the cause of the stress is reduced, you're left with all these chemicals still trying to help you fight or run away. That's often what makes you feel shaky. I'm sure that if you're in a customer service job you're very much aware of how stressful dealing with the public can be. Digging a hole in the ground or any other physical work may be tiring, but brain work can be mentally and physically exhausting. So you need to be in good physical and mental health to deal with all of this.

You may be thinking that there is not much you can do about the stress and the drain on your brain energy. We looked earlier at thinking and not reacting. Reacting drains the brain; thinking less so. The reacting behaviour programmes, such as defiant, controlling or passive, drain the brain. The thinking programme does not.

Say, for example, a customer calls to say:

'You've sent me the wrong order. This isn't what I ordered. It's totally useless to me and so are you!'

If you react internally with:

'Oh no, what a disaster. This customer is going crazy and I don't know what to say. He's really mad and he's stressing me out.'

All this is coming from your passive programme and it will stress you out! Switch to your thinking programme and say to yourself:

> 'Okay, I have an angry customer on the line. I can understand why he's angry and I will use all my skills to deal with this.'

Do not, and I repeat, do not, use the 'Oh no' words. Every time you say: 'Oh no' to yourself, your brain experiences a huge drain of energy.

If you have a job that involves managing difficult people, then as well as using your thinking programme you need to have other things you can do. Going home and slumping in front of the TV and whingeing to your partner won't help the brain energy. Many people do other negative things that are ineffective. They smoke too much, drink or eat too much. Sometimes you have to push yourself into other activities that have huge benefits for your brain energy. Here are some of my suggestions but I'm sure you can think of lots more:

- Play sport.

- Watch sport.

- Play music.

- Listen to music.

- Take up a hobby.

- Go swimming.

- Mix with friends.

- Have a laugh.

- Make love.

- Learn to dance.

Remember, stop the negative stuff – it'll kill you!

Body energy

I'm sure that you're well aware by now that, if you eat too much, eat the wrong things, smoke too much or drink too much alcohol, then your body is in danger of breaking down. If you want to be successful in managing difficult people, and your life, then you're going to have to look after your body. If you look better and feel fitter, then you will have much more confidence to manage difficult people.

I often look at people in the street and they look so dull – poor skin, dull hair and overweight. I have friends in their 40s and 50s and 60s and they look fantastic. Feeling good physically will give you more confidence to choose your behaviour programme and manage difficult people. It's important to look after your teeth with a regular visit to the dentist and also have your eyes tested on a regular basis. If you don't want to go to the gym, then that's okay, but you need to find some other kind of exercise that pushes up the heart rate and makes you sweat a little.

A couple of years ago I decided to learn to dance the tango. It's good exercise, lots of fun and I met some new people. I like to eat all kinds of food and I like to drink beer and wine. But I certainly want to look after my body and ensure it lasts and works well for as long as possible. I recommend you do the same.

4 RAPPORT

To be really good at managing difficult people, you need to learn and apply the magic of rapport. I say magic because if you develop that skill you will make your life so much easier.

At the time of writing this, I received a phone call from my friend John. He was telling me about a recent trip to the airport, taking his mother and father to their holiday flight. The check-in time was 6.20am and John and his parents arrived at 6am. John noticed two women sitting behind the check-in desk having a chat. He approached one of them and asked if it would be possible to check the bags even though they were 20 minutes early. He received a curt 'No' and was told to print off a boarding pass at one of the machines. This annoyed John, not so much because he couldn't check in, but more about how he was spoken to. He also knew that his elderly parents would have difficulties using the machine and he was glad he was there to help.

The woman at the check-in desk has almost no rapport-building skills. She possibly was unable to check John's parents in due to technical reasons, but these weren't explained. Her response was a straight 'No'. John, as the customer, is likely to interpret her response as a lack of willingness to be flexible and helpful. In a customer service situation the answer often is 'No'; however, it's how you say the word 'No' that matters. This check-in clerk is setting herself up to receive lots of difficult customers.

In order to minimise the number of difficult people you have to deal with or to improve your ability to manage them, you need to be good at building rapport. Rapport is not just about speaking to other people, it's about listening and understanding how the other person sees the situation. It's also about being able to empathise and appreciate how they feel.

There's a story about three people taking a walk through a beautiful forest. One of them is an artist, the other a botanist and the third person works in the timber business. As they walk through the forest, the artist is thinking:

'What a beautiful forest, look at those stunning views! I'd love to come back here some day and capture this scene in a picture.'

The botanist is walking through the forest with her nose to the ground, and she's thinking:

'I've never seen so many wonderful plants – I'd like to spend more time studying them.'

The guy who works in the timber business is examining every tree and thinking:

'There are some wonderful woods growing here. I could chop this lot down and make a fortune.'

We all see the world in a different way. The person with good rapport skills understands this and thinks about it when communicating with other people. Good rapport-building skills are about conveying to the other person that you see the world in the same way they see it. I use this saying when I'm running a sales course:

'People buy from people, and they buy from people who are just like themselves.'

NLP

You may have heard of NLP (neuro-linguistic programming). It is one of the fastest-growing developments in applied psychology. NLP practitioners talk about mirroring and matching the behaviour of other people. It's not about mimicking others; it's more about behaving as they do, making them feel that you have good rapport with them. Many people do this naturally. Let me give you an example.

Let's say that you had just met some friends and they had a small child with them. You would stand and talk with your friends in an adult manner. When they introduced you to the child you'd probably squat down to the child's level, speak more softly and with a more child-like voice. In other words, you don't use the same words, tone of voice or body language with the child as you would do with the adults.

When interacting with adults, it improves your ability to build rapport if you match the other person's words, tone and body language. Say, for example, you were dealing with someone who spoke fairly quietly and slowly. It would improve your rapport building if you spoke quietly and slowly. Your natural style may be to speak quickly and loudly, but that will not improve your rapport-building skills.

One of the other factors highlighted by NLP is that we all have a sensory preference when we communicate with other people. There are the visual people who are more influenced by what they see. The auditory people are more influenced by what comes in through their ears. And then there are the kinaesthetic people who are more concerned by how something feels. There are also olfactory people who are primarily influenced by smell and gustatory people who are influenced by taste; however, these kinds of people are less common.

Most of us communicate from our visual, auditory or kinaesthetic senses. Visual people will say things like: 'I see what you mean' or 'This looks good to me'. Whereas an auditory person would say: 'I hear what you're saying' or 'This sound good to me'. The kinaesthetic person would say: 'I get a good feeling about this' or 'This feels good to me'.

To build rapport with another person, it makes sense to use their sensory preference. To a visual person you might say: 'Show me what you mean.' If you observed that the person you were interacting with was an auditory person, it would be better to say: 'Tell me what you mean.' If you were aware that you were with a kinaesthetic person, you would say: 'Can you demonstrate what you mean?'

If you want to get better at identifying the different preferences, think about yourself or those closest to you. For example, I am very visual and kinaesthetic. I know this because I'm not particularly interested in music. I own about six CDs and I've only ever been to two music concerts in my life. I'd far rather watch a film or see some kind of production in the theatre. I'm interested in art, and I always spot friends in the street before they see me. If you want to explain something to me, it's best to show me a drawing or something written down. My kinaesthetic side is satisfied if you let me get my hands on something. People who are not highly auditory are also not particularly good readers of books. This is because when we read we tend to talk to ourselves inside our brain, so reading is more of an auditory sense than a visual one.

When I'm conducting training workshops I usually ask people to read some text and discuss what they've read with the group; this satisfies the auditory people. I show a video or slides for the visual people, and I organise group exercises so that the kinaesthetic people can feel what's being taught.

I just want to say a few words about people who are highly olfactory. You can spot these people in the supermarket. When they buy products like washing-up liquid or detergent, they often take the lid off and smell the product. Other people may regard this as unusual because they're more concerned with whether the product works than how it smells.

To build good rapport with people, find out what their sensory preference is and communicate to them from that level.

Get interested

Successful people are excellent at building rapport. I've met several in my time and I'm always impressed by their interest in me. Observe all the people you meet on a day-to-day basis and practise your rapport-building skills. Speak with everyone you come into contact with. I'm often disappointed by the way people react to the checkout staff at my local supermarket. The checkout person usually says 'Hello' or 'Good morning', and receives just a grunt in return. When they tell the customer the bill total, I've seen the customer hand over their credit card and leave the checkout without a word. I always make a point of at least passing the time of day and it's great to see the response from the person at the checkout. All of this is good practice for when you meet, and have to manage, the difficult person.

5 Courage

This is about the courage to take action. If you are to become better at managing difficult people, you need the courage to run your own mind and change your behaviour programme. It goes without saying that you need courage to face up to and manage the difficult person. It's often the case that you put off dealing with that person because you don't like confrontation. You also fear that it won't make any difference. This book will give you practical things to say and more confidence to approach a difficult person. But you need to get your internal conversations going and talk to yourself in a positive way.

'Courage is the first of human qualities because it is the quality which guarantees all others.' – Winston Churchill (1874–1965, British statesman, Prime Minister)

Many managers ignore poor behaviour in their staff because they believe that it might result in conflict and de-motivate them. What then happens is that the staff member continues to behave badly, the other team members get de-motivated and the customers and the business suffer. Managers need courage to deal with these difficult staff members, and do it as soon as possible. This will make their lives easier and reduce the levels of stress. When faced with a difficult situation, listen to your internal conversations and ask yourself:

'Is this decision I'm making the best one for me?'

If the answer is 'No', then change it.

Remember my story about being shy and asking for a date with the girl of my dreams. It took a lot of courage for me to do that but, at the end of the day, I was glad I did.

Feel the fear

If you find yourself lacking courage to do something or deal with a difficult situation, ask yourself: 'What will be the result of not doing this?' You'll come back with an answer such as:

▓ The problem will continue.

▓ Other people will think I'm a wimp.

▓ I'll always be taken advantage of.

▓ I'll still be afraid.

▓ I'll feel bad about myself.

▓ I'll regret it later.

Then ask yourself: 'What will be the result of doing something about this?'

▓ I'll feel better.

▓ The problem will be resolved.

▓ And if not, I'll be glad I approached it.

▓ Other people will admire me.

▓ I'll be less likely to be taken advantage of.

I'd be nervous if I wasn't nervous

Dealing with a difficult person may make you nervous. I know that I always had butterflies in my stomach when I was about to face a difficult customer or staff member. Let me give you some thoughts on nervousness.

When I run a presentation skills seminar, people inevitably talk about nervousness and the courage to get up and speak.

I'm sure that you've heard people say: 'I could never get up and speak in front of a group.' Public speaking is apparently one of our biggest fears. What it basically boils down to is the fear of making a fool of yourself and being ridiculed.

In the seminar I go on to explain how being nervous is a good thing. The nerves, or the fear, cause all those stress chemicals to flood through your system to deal with whatever is attacking you. These chemicals will make your brain sharper, give you more energy and make you better equipped to deliver a great presentation. When you're nervous about dealing with a difficult person these chemicals will again equip you to deal with the situation. Fear is good, but only as long as you are aware of it and keep it under control – that's what courage is all about. Winston Churchill says that courage is the first of human qualities and who am I to argue.

There is no doubt that successful business people must have the courage to challenge their own programming and deal with difficult customer and staff situations. They need courage to do things in a different way and challenge conventional wisdom. They also need the courage of their own convictions and not to allow other people to run their mind.

Two men used to leave their office every night and walk together to the bus stop. On the way, one of the men would stop and buy a newspaper from a news stand at the side of the road. The old man who ran the news stand was always grumpy and ill mannered. However, the man who bought the newspaper was always polite and courteous to the old man. One evening the man's friend said:

'I don't understand why you're always so polite and courteous to that guy, he's always so rude.'

The other man replied:

'I will not allow that man's behaviour to decide mine. I will always decide my own behaviour and I'll always treat him with courtesy and respect. How he behaves is up to him.'

Successful business people must have the courage to challenge themselves and accept that they may not always be right. They need to listen to other people, study new ways of doing things – and think!

There is a book by Susan Jeffers titled *Feel the Fear and Do It Anyway*. That's what I advise you to do.

4

Prevention Is Better than Cure

'There's no such thing as bad weather, only the wrong clothes.'
– Billy Connolly (1942–, Scottish comedian, musician, actor)

It is inevitable that you'll have to manage a difficult person sometime in your life and, as I said before, if you're in a customer-contact job dealing with the public every day, then your chances are probably higher than a farmer tending his livestock. Just like many things in this life, taking preventative action is much better than suffering the consequences of not. Do you go to the dentist regularly? You do that because you want to have a charming smile and also because you don't want to suffer the pain of toothache and losing all your teeth. It's the same when dealing with other people – if we can improve our communication skills it can make our lives so much easier.

Do you remember the story I told earlier about the clerk at the airline check-in desk? Her lack of good communication skills will ensure that she meets lots of difficult people. Now, I'm not suggesting that you are that person and you probably believe you communicate really well with other people. Nevertheless, you may be inadvertently saying or doing things that may exacerbate a situation and increase your probability of having to deal with difficult people.

Let's look at some factors that will minimise your likelihood of having to manage a difficult person.

COMMUNICATE ON A HUMAN/BUSINESS LEVEL

Communicating with another person can take place on two levels: the human level and the business level. Any communication will certainly take place on a business level. Buying a bar of chocolate in a shop requires business-level communication: 'I'd like a bar of fruit and nut chocolate, please' or in the office: 'Mary, please type this report for me and return it to me this afternoon.' These business-level interactions would be so much better if you add a human level.

I'd like you to think for a moment about a time when you experienced really exceptional customer service. Perhaps it was when you booked a holiday, dealt with a utility company or bought something in a shop or a store. Think about it for a moment and write down what made this service so good. When I do this exercise with a group of people, they can always tell me all the bad stories but they often find difficulty in thinking of a positive customer service story. People eventually come forward with examples of good service, saying things like:

▨   The person who dealt with me was really kind.

▓ They listened to me.

▓ They made me feel important.

▓ They went out of their way.

▓ They were very friendly.

▓ They used my name.

Occasionally some people will say:

▓ The service was fast.

▓ They delivered on time.

▓ The product or service did what they said it would.

The first group of answers always outweighs the second group. In other words, people make decisions about the level of customer service based on the interactions they have with the people in the business. These are human-level responses. The comments in the second group are business-level responses and are taken as a given. We expect goods or services to be delivered on time and to do what the supplier said they would.

In a similar situation, if I ask participants in a seminar to describe a job that they enjoyed and what made it a good place to work, they rarely say things like:

▓ I was well paid.

▓ The working conditions were excellent.

▓ We had a first-class staff restaurant.

▓ I attended some great training courses.

▓ I felt I had job security.

They are more likely to say:

▓ My boss always listened to me.

▓ He made me feel my comments had value.

▓ He was firm but fair.

▓ My manager told me when I did something well.

▓ She helped me when I hadn't done something well.

▓ She told me what was happening in the company.

▓ I had some great colleagues and we worked well together as a team.

All of these comments in the second list are human-level responses.

When interacting with other people, human-level responses are vitally important. It doesn't matter if it's face to face, over the phone or by e-mail, we need to mix the human with the business. People often say to me:

> 'I don't have time for all this nicey-nicey, touchy-feely stuff. I need to get the job done.'

My answer to this is:

> 'If you introduce some human-level responses with the people
> you interact with, be they customers or staff, then you will get
> the job done, better and faster, with less mistakes.'

This isn't about being nicey-nicey; it's about meeting the
human needs of every person you interact with. Human
beings are almost totally driven by their emotions.

So what does this mean in practical terms? When dealing with
another person, you intersperse some human comments with
the business comments. Let me give you an example. A few
years ago my wife and I were looking to buy a house in the
Yorkshire area of England. One day, after a morning's house
hunting, we entered a village pub. The landlord behind the
bar greeted us with:

> 'Good afternoon, Sir, good afternoon, Madam. What can I get
> you today?'

> 'We'd like some lunch please, and something to drink.'

> 'Certainly, Sir, I'll get the menu for you. Meanwhile, what would
> you like to drink?'

> 'I'd like a beer and my wife would like an orange juice please.'

He proceeded to pour the drinks and interspersed what he
was doing with:

> 'Have you come far today? Are you on holiday?'

I explained that we were looking for a house in the area. While pouring the drinks and organising the menu, he told us about places to visit and gave us some tips on buying a house in the area. He was a really nice guy and we warmed to this pub and the area.

Let's imagine that I found a problem with the food that was served to us for lunch or the time taken to serve it. It would have been very difficult to be angry with the landlord. I would probably have approached him in my thinking programme and I'm sure he would have been receptive to my complaint. On the other hand, if he had been a surly and uncommunicative landlord, then I would probably have approached him in my controlling or defiant programme and he would have found himself dealing with a difficult customer!

There is a saying:

'We get the customers we deserve.'

When we interact with other people, whether it's a difficult person or not, it's important to open the conversation on a human level.

The best managers that I ever worked for were the ones who showed an interest in me as a person. I can think of one sales manager in particular who always opened every phone conversation by asking about my wife or how my holiday was or any other situation that may have been concerning me. Let me assure you, this manager was no soft touch – he knew what he wanted and he made sure that I knew. He needed me to deliver more sales and I always did my best for him. I knew that he would always treat me fairly.

Communicating on a human level increases your likeability and improves your success in managing difficult people. There are also other ways to increase your likeability factor – let's consider some of them.

BUILDING YOUR LIKEABILITY FACTOR

Why do you think Barack Obama overwhelmingly won the US presidential election? Perhaps it was because of his policies for change or even the amount of money invested in his campaign. Or perhaps it was his ability to express eloquently the hopes, answers and beliefs of a good chunk of the American people. Some people may even say that Obama was a better bet than his rival, John McCain. I think it is probably a mixture of all these reasons, and a few more. But more than anything else, I believe he has a high likeability factor.

So what's likeability got to do with anything? Surely we're going to vote for the policies not the person? Somehow I don't think so! What many politicians tend to forget is that we voters are humans and the thing about humans is that they'll always be driven by their emotions, not their logic. We let our heart rule our head all the time. If we decide that we don't like someone, then we have a heck of a job believing anything they say. How well our politicians score on the likeability factor is going to influence whether we believe them or not.

Roger Ailes (1940–), media consultant to Presidents Nixon, Reagan and Bush Snr, wrote:

> *'The silver bullet in business and politics is the like factor. All things being equal, we are more likely to vote for people we feel we like.'*

However, so many of our politicians seem totally unconcerned by this. Consider some other public figures that have been affected by the like factor. Bill Clinton came through some difficult situations relatively unscathed – the reason being that the American public quite liked him. Margaret Thatcher suffered more than she needed because too many people didn't like her. Princess Diana's funeral gave a clear indication of how many people liked her. I don't believe we would have seen the same outpouring of public grief had that tragic accident happened to another member of the Royal Family.

The likeability factor also affects products and the organisations that supply them. As with people, it's not so much about what the product does but rather do we like the brand? Some years ago Procter & Gamble launched Ariel to compete against Persil. All the tests proved that Ariel washed whiter, but Persil remained the top brand. P&G managers tore their hair out looking for an explanation, until one day someone told them: 'Well, I believe people quite like Persil.'

If your likeability factor is high, votes go up, sales go up, you go up and you'll have less difficult people to manage.

But what about the other people in your life: are they likeable? What about your boss, your dentist or your accountant? I get some funny looks when I tell people that I've no idea if my accountant is any good or not. How would I know if he is a good accountant? I'm not competent to judge. I only know that I like and trust him, and that means he'll continue to get my business.

Warren Buffett (1930–), Chairman of Berkshire Hathaway and sometimes acclaimed as the world's greatest investor, once said:

> *'I've walked away from some great deals because I didn't like the people I was dealing with.'*

Harry Redknapp took over as manager of struggling soccer team Tottenham Hotspur. Redknapp engineered a remarkable turnaround in a short period of time. I believe that a great deal of his success is down to his high likeability factor. Phil Neville (1977–), the former Everton, Manchester United and England footballer, recently commented:

> *'If the players like you then that decides 95% of your success as a manager.'*

So how do we get this likeability factor if we haven't got it? Or how do we improve it if we have, and what's it all about anyway? Well, as far as companies are concerned, it's all about whether we trust them and feel that they care about us when we contact them. Do they have the human touch? The advertising agencies know all about the likeability factor and the human touch. They want to make us laugh. They use cute children and animals. They feature celebrities that we like and can relate to. Andrex TV ads certainly aren't about what you can do with toilet paper; they're more about puppies and children.

Some commercial organisations still don't quite understand this. The high street banks in the UK were once criticised in a report that suggested many customers didn't like their bank. One senior manager replied in the press saying: 'We continue to grow our business because our products and services meet customer demand and expectation.' He fails to realise that it's not just about products and services – it's about the human things, like dropping into your local branch and having a talk with the manager. It's much harder to do that nowadays, which is one of the main reasons for poor reports in customer satisfaction surveys.

Likeability is about being human; it's about displaying warmth. Bill Clinton displays warmth; Hillary Clinton less so. Being known as the Prince of Darkness doesn't suggest too much warmth in UK politician Peter Mandelson. Richard Branson has warmth and so did Princess Diana. Nelson Mandela had it. Margaret Thatcher didn't display it in her time as Prime Minister.

Likeability in people is also measured by their ability to really listen and be interested in others. Likeable people use your name and look as if they care. We like people who have something positive to say and don't whinge! Likeable people empathise with our problems and accept that we may have a different view of the world from them. Likeability is demonstrated by a genuine smile, good eye contact, a sense of humour and relaxed open body language. Whether in our personal or working lives, people judge us by what we say and what we do. However, more importantly, people's opinions are influenced by how likeable we are. Trying to communicate with a difficult person, to be likeable and to get them to accept your point of view can be a real challenge. Your ability to sell yourself will make that process so much easier.

> 'If you would win a man to your cause, first convince him that you are his sincere friend.' – Abraham Lincoln

Here are some other factors that will minimise the possibility of having to manage a difficult person.

DON'T GET HOOKED

I'm about to tell you a little story so make yourself comfortable. Have you ever been fishing? I'm not a fan myself but I'm sure that you understand the basic principle. You attach a piece of bait to a hook and dangle it in the water. What then happens is that some unsuspecting fish comes along, bites the bait, ends up on the hook and you reel it in.

Let's just go back a few steps. As the fish is swimming around, it is totally in control of its own destiny. It can swim anywhere it likes and it can eat anything it fancies. When it's confronted with the fisherman's bait, it has the choice whether to bite or not. If it decides not to take the bait, it can swim on its merry way and live its life to the full. 'But it's a fish,' you say, 'and it'll probably take the bait.' When it does, that's the fish in trouble. Instead of being in charge of its own destiny, the fisherman is now in charge. The fish will get stressed and will probably lose its life.

Of course, you're not a fish, but other people, difficult people, will try to get you on the line, they'll try to hook you. This is not something they do consciously. However, by what they say, what they do and how they look, they are dangling bait in front of you. If you choose to take that bait, then the difficult person is in charge of your behaviour.

Have you heard people say things such as:

■ 'She makes me really mad!' (Hooked)

■ 'His behaviour really annoys me.' (Hooked)

■ 'How dare she speak to me like that!' (Hooked)

■ 'If he thinks I'm just going to do what he wants . . . !' (Hooked)

■ 'How could she come in here dressed like that!' (Hooked)

The behaviour of these people potentially hooks you into your controlling, defiant or passive programme.

In Chapter 6, I'll show you things to do and say that will help to prevent you from getting hooked. But for the moment, remember: you choose your behaviour programme – 'Don't get hooked!'

'If I had kept my mouth shut, I wouldn't be here.' – Sign under a mounted fish.

SOME WORDS ARE BETTER THAN OTHERS

You probably realise how the wrong tone of voice and negative body language can cause problems when dealing with other people, particularly customers and staff. However, using the wrong language can also make a difficult situation worse.

There are certain trigger words that cause people to become more difficult, especially in emotionally charged situations, and they should be avoided. They tend to be words from your controlling, defiant and passive programmes. They include:

■ 'Have to' – as in: 'You'll have to speak to the sales department yourself.'

■ 'I can't' or 'You can't' – as in: 'I can't do anything about that' or 'You can't do that.'

■ 'I'll try' – as in: 'I'll try to speak to the finance department today.'

■ 'But' – as in: 'I agree with what you're saying but . . .'

■ 'Sorry' – as in: 'I'm sorry 'bout that.'

'Have to', 'Don't' and 'Can't'

'Have to', 'don't' and 'can't' are words from your controlling programme that annoy people. They are often words that hook people. They are inflammatory and are best left out of any interactions, especially with difficult people. Imagine how you feel when someone says to you:

■ 'You'll have to phone a different number.'

■ 'You'll have to come back later.'

■ 'I can't help you with that.'

■ 'I don't have time to speak to you now.'

■ 'You'll have to get that finished today.'

You might ask yourself:

'Why does this always happen to me?'

Or you might think:

'Why doesn't somebody let me know that the extensions have changed? Besides, I don't have to do anything. They're not my boss. Just wait till they call me looking for help.'

'I need you to . . .' and 'Have to'

The statement 'I need you to . . .' can come across as manipulative, which again is behaviour from your controlling programme. It says to the other person:

'I don't care about you – I only care about what I need.'

Instead of the words 'have to' or 'I need you to', why not try:

'Are you willing to . . .'

Or just a straight:

'Will you . . .'

'Can't'

'Can't' can be replaced with:

'I'm unable to because . . .'

'I'll try'

The phrase 'I'll try' comes across as submissive and can invite the controlling behaviour programme from the other person. Some people hear these words as a commitment and expect you to do what you say. More often, people will hear it as something you probably won't do. 'I'll try' is very wishy-washy. It can be replaced with something more honest:

'This is what I can do' or 'This is what I'm unable to do.'

'But'

Instead of using 'But . . .' with difficult people, it's a good idea to use:

'However'

When you substitute 'however', you'll provide a smoother and more positive transition to new information, options or alternatives. You could also use 'and' instead of 'but.' For example:

'I understand your situation and the reason I'm unable to do
what you ask is . . .'

Instead of saying 'but', you could leave it out altogether. For
example, instead of:

'I agree with what you're saying, but I can't help you.'

use:

'I agree with what you're saying. The reason I'm unable to help
you is . . .'

Jargon

Any forms of jargon are best avoided. Every organisation
has its jargon. I often ask seminar participants for examples
of jargon in their organisation and they find this difficult.
This is because, subconsciously, they believe that everyone
understands their jargon. When we use technical terms, buzz
words or acronyms, the other person may not understand.
They may also feel that you are talking down to them, which
makes them feel patronised and uncomfortable. Without
over-simplifying or speaking to the other person as if they
were an idiot, it's far better to use words that the other person
is comfortable with and understands.

On a recent workshop that I was running for some telecom
engineers, I would listen to their chat at the coffee breaks.
When they were talking to each other about work-based
matters, I hadn't a clue what they were saying. This is
acceptable in this situation, but if they were speaking to a

customer using this language then it could make life more difficult for them.

'Sorry'

'Sorry' is an overused word. It comes from your passive programme. Everyone says it when something goes wrong and it has lost its value.

I was checking out of a hotel one morning after a poor night's sleep. There had been some construction work going on in the building next to the hotel and the noise had gone on for most of the night. When the checkout clerk said:

'Did you have a good evening, Mr Fairweather?'

I told her about my disturbed night. I didn't whinge and I didn't complain but I suggested they may want to warn guests about the potential noise. She said:

'Oh, sorry 'bout that. What credit card do you want to use to pay your bill?'

She didn't look sorry or concerned, and I got the impression that she just wanted to process my checkout and get me out the door. It would have been better to lose the sorry word and say something like:

'I apologise for that, Mr Fairweather.'

If you really need to use the sorry word, it's far better to use it as part of a whole sentence:

> 'I'm sorry your sleep was disturbed, Mr Fairweather. Next time you visit us, please ask for a quiet room and we'll do our best to provide it.'

You will often hear someone say:

> 'Sorry to have kept you waiting.'

This statement comes from your passive programme and invites controlling from the other person. They might say:

> 'So you should be sorry – I've been waiting for ages.'

Far better to say:

> 'Thank you for waiting, Mr Brown. I now have the information you want.'

This comes from your thinking programme and is more likely to invite a reasonable response from the other person. There are other things you can say instead of 'sorry' and we'll come on to those in Chapter 6.

'Calm down'

'Calm down' is something you should definitely avoid saying to a difficult person. It comes from your controlling programme and will invite a controlling or defiant response.

'It's company policy'

'It's company policy' is another phrase that can make a difficult situation worse. If you say to a customer:

'I can't help because it's company policy.'

they will interpret this as:

'You're just using this as an excuse not to help me.'

It's far better to say what the company policy is:

'I'm unable to help you, and the reason is that giving you the information you've asked for would be a security risk for both you and our company.'

At the end of the day the answer to a difficult person could be 'No'. However, choosing your words more carefully will have a more positive effect on how he or she reacts and ultimately responds to you.

In the 1993 film *Falling Down* Michael Douglas plays an unemployed, divorced engineer who wants to visit his daughter on her birthday. He encounters various levels of harassment on his journey and eventually he cracks! One scene takes place in the Whammy Burger fast food restaurant. When Michael's character orders the breakfast, he's told: 'It's too late, you can't have the breakfast.' Michael calls for the manager and is then told: 'It's not our policy, you have to order from the lunch menu.' This sends Michael completely over the edge – he brings out a machine gun from his bag and starts terrorising the staff and customers. I'm not saying that someone is going to shoot you for using the wrong words, but it will definitely make them more difficult to deal with than they were before.

People sometimes feel that changing language is over-simplifying matters. But if you're managing a difficult person, then you need all the help you can get. Using more appropriate words will make your life so much easier.

DON'T LET PET PEEVES HOOK YOU

When I'm running a Managing Difficult People seminar, I ask the participants to make a list of the pet peeves they have about other people. Some of the participants are reluctant to admit their pet peeves. They believe they shouldn't have any or they're too embarrassed to admit to them. With a bit of encouragement from me, and some of the more outspoken members of the group, we eventually end up with a huge list on the flip chart. People will talk about things that irritate them about other people and drive them crazy, things they disapprove of, find embarrassing or just don't like. Here are some of the pet peeves I've heard from seminar participants:

- Speaking with your mouth full

- Bad breath

- Body odour

- Not saying please or thank you
- General bad manners
- Answering a mobile phone in the middle of a conversation
- Squeezing the toothpaste from the wrong end
- Putting a toilet roll on the holder the wrong way around
- Untidiness
- Bad timekeeping
- Smoking
- Obesity
- Drunkenness
- Not looking you in the eye
- Eating too fast or too slow
- Slurping food or drink
- Not listening
- Loud music
- Loud people

As you see, the list goes on and on. Once we have all these pet peeves on the flip chart, I then ask the group to vote on each one. In a group of let's say 20 people, 12 might say 'speaking with your mouth full' is a pet peeve for them. Another six people might say 'untidiness' is a peeve for them. What comes out of this is that not all of us have the same pet peeves. If you consistently arrive late, you might drive some people crazy, while others don't really care if you're late or not.

Most pet peeves come from your controlling programme. You probably learned them from your parents and the people you grew up with. When I was a child, I was never allowed to waste food. I had to eat everything that was on my plate before I could leave the table. This programming is so strong that as an adult I admit to being a bit peeved by people who pick at their food and leave a lot on the plate without eating it.

When interacting with other people, it is highly possible that we allow our pet peeves to influence that interaction. I was running a seminar for some bank employees and several of them stated the same pet peeve. They hate it when a customer answers their mobile phone in the middle of a transaction or conversation. Because the bank employee finds this behaviour annoying, it could potentially affect how he or she deals with the customer. The staff member's annoyance, albeit slight, may be transmitted to a customer by tone of voice or body language. It is then possible that the customer may become difficult. Any customer's behaviour, which is a pet peeve for you, may hook you into your controlling programme and that will potentially cause problems.

The other aspect of this is that, although we all have pet peeves, what may not be a problem for you may be a pet peeve for the other person. You may think that being a bit late with your report is not such a big deal, but the other person might and that could cause them to be difficult.

THE WAY YOU SEE IT MAY NOT BE THE WAY IT IS

In any interaction between people, there will always be:

The way they see it – The way you see it – The way it is.

Take the example of Dave who usually arrives about 10 to 15 minutes late for a meeting. The way he sees it is:

'We're supposed to meet at 8am and I'm here just after that. I don't suppose anyone expects me to be here dead on 8 o'clock.'

The way you see it is:

'Dave is so selfish, he just shows up whenever it suits him. I've been here since 7.45 so that we can start at 8 o'clock. He has no respect for me or any of his colleagues.'

The way it is: Dave arrived at 8.12am.

Your controlling programme tells you that people should show up early or dead on time for a meeting. Dave's fun programme tells him that 'It's only a meeting. It'll be boring anyway, so we'll try to have a laugh and I'll get there when I get there!'

I'm the person who always turns up early for an appointment, be it business or pleasure. I have friends who are like me and always turn up on time, and I have other friends who arrive just when they're ready. At one time I might have allowed this to annoy me, to be a pet peeve, but now I switch to my thinking programme. I realise that this is the way these friends are and in no way does it make them any less of a friend.

Behaving from your controlling, passive or defiant programme can be stressful for you; it is self-inflicted stress. You are allowing yourself to be stressed because other people do not behave in a way you have been programmed to believe.

I once went out with a girl who I was very keen on. However, I didn't like the direct, in-your-face way she would talk to me. In my family we would regard this as a bit rude. When I eventually met her family, I discovered that they all spoke to each other in a similar manner. That didn't make them any less caring, helpful or kind; it was just the way they had been programmed to behave.

So you may find yourself having to manage a difficult person, mainly because they see the world differently from you. If you say to someone: 'I'll phone you back in a couple of minutes', you may intend to phone them back when you have all the information. That could be within ten minutes, thirty minutes, one hour or the next two hours. On hearing that you'll phone back in a couple of minutes, the other person may sit by the phone waiting for it to ring. When it doesn't, they phone you back in a negative frame of mind and you then have a difficult person to deal with.

Personal relationships often come to grief because of this inability to see it the way the other person does. A man may stop for a drink with his friends after work and phone his wife to say that he will be home later. She translates 'later' as perhaps 8 to 9 pm. But he believes 'later' is 'You'll see me when you see me'. Guess what happens?

The point has been made several times that we are all different. How often have you been to a play or a movie and thoroughly enjoyed it, whereas the person you were with didn't enjoy it at all. You think: 'What's wrong with them? They must be stupid or perhaps they're just being difficult.'

When someone doesn't see things the way you do, there is potential for you to get stressed and collect negative feelings. What then happens is that you dump these negative feelings on the other person, and then you have a difficult situation. The way to avoid these negative feelings is to:

▪ Accept people the way they are.

▪ Decide not to react to other people's behaviour.

▪ Be responsible for your own feelings.

▪ Change your expectations.

▪ Ask for help when you need it.

▪ Communicate from your thinking programme.

There is a lot you can do to minimise the number of difficult
people you have to manage. Fire prevention is a much better
course of action than fire fighting. However, fires will break
out and behaving assertively will minimise the damage.

5

Choose to Be Assertive

IS ASSERTIVENESS GOOD OR BAD?

If I was to describe someone to you and I said: 'She's a very assertive lady', how do you think you would feel towards that person? Can I suggest that you may not feel comfortable having to deal with that individual. I sometimes hear people being described as 'really assertive' and it's often the wrong description. They're usually describing someone who is behaving from their controlling programme, and that is aggressive not assertive.

Assertive communication can make all the difference to your personal success and your ability to manage difficult people. It's more than just learning to talk in a different way. It's about:

Thinking positively – Feeling confident – Behaving
assertively

To develop your assertiveness, you don't have to change your personality – only your behaviour and thoughts. In assertiveness training we talk about submissive, aggressive and assertive behaviour. Submissive and aggressive behaviour relates to your inbuilt fight or flight programmes that rescue you from problem situations. Assertive behaviour will help you communicate clearly and confidently your needs, wants and feelings to other people without abusing in any way their human rights. It is more positive, it will produce better results when managing a difficult person and it can be learned.

Let's look more closely at each type of behaviour.

Submissive (flight)

Submissive behaviour comes from your passive programme. It is natural behaviour and, depending on your upbringing, you may develop it throughout your life. People who are dominant in this programme tend to:

- Avoid stating their needs and feelings.

- Communicate their needs and feelings in an apologetic way.

- Give others rights that they don't take for themselves.

Submissive behaviour sounds like this:

> 'I'm really sorry. I just don't have the time to go through those reports with you just now. I've got to get all these accounts finished before lunchtime. My boss is a real pain, asking me to do this today. I'd really like to help you. I'll look at it later if that's okay.'

Aggressive (fight)

This comes from your defiant or controlling programmes. Again, this is an inbuilt programme that can be developed throughout your life. If we learn that we can achieve things by using our controlling programme, we continue to develop it. Naturally, this is to the detriment of our relationships with other people. People who are aggressive tend to:

▦   Encourage others to do things by flattery or manipulation.

▦   Ignore the needs and feelings of others, either intentionally or by default.

▦   Take rights for themselves that they don't give to others.

Aggressive behaviour sounds like this:

> 'Do you think I've nothing better to do than check those reports?'

> *'There are two people in the world that are not likeable: a master and a slave.'* – Nikki Giovanni (1943–, American poet)

Assertive

This comes from your thinking programme and, although it may be natural for a few people, it tends to be learned behaviour. It's about:

▦   Being clear and direct in what you say.

▦   Stating your needs and feelings in a straightforward way.

▓   Standing up for your rights without violating the rights of others.

Assertive behaviour sounds like this:

> 'I'm unable to help you with those reports this morning. I am doing accounts at the moment and I'll be pleased to help you this afternoon. What time suits you?'

None of this is good or bad; it's just the way we are. But if we want to be better at managing difficult people, we need to ensure that:

▓   We don't use passive or aggressive behaviour.

▓   We recognise passive or aggressive behaviour in others.

▓   We learn and use assertive techniques with difficult people.

EXERCISING YOUR RIGHTS

I've mentioned the word 'rights' a few times so let's take a closer look at your rights.

▓   **You have the right to feel the way you do, to have needs and opinions, and have them respected by others.** You have the right not to justify yourself to other people. We all see the world in different ways.

▨ **You have the right to say no.** When you consider your own needs, it may be that you have to refuse other people's requests for help. It is far better to refuse a request politely than to lead the other person on and then find an excuse to refuse.

▨ **You have the right to consider yourself.** You do not have to consider yourself over other people but it is important to consider your own needs in relation to other people.

▨ **You have the right to ask but not to demand.** We sometimes tend to beat about the bush when we want something from someone else. We drop hints and veiled comments to soften the request. It's far better to say what you have to say and ask for what you want. It's fairer and much more effective.

▨ **You have the right to be successful.** It doesn't matter what you do, you must acknowledge your achievements no matter how trivial they are. If you have just dealt positively with a difficult customer or staff member, acknowledge your success.

▨ **You have the right to choose any of your behaviour programmes.** You can decide not to assert yourself and stand up for your rights. It's important to know that you have the confidence and self-esteem to assert yourself whenever you wish.

▨ **You have the right not to understand.** Too often, people fail to ask for clarification believing that they will look stupid or foolish. The only way you'll learn is by admitting your lack of knowledge and asking questions. Other people will more often respect you for your honesty.

■ **You have the right to make a mistake.** The majority of people feel really uncomfortable and cringe when they believe they have said or done the wrong thing. It's important to remember that no one is perfect and that making a mistake doesn't make you a stupid or incompetent person. Remember, the person who never made a mistake never made anything.

■ **You have the right to change your mind.** Many people worry that changing their mind is a sign of weakness. Just think for a moment of all the politicians who avoid admitting to a change of mind. It is often the case that you change your mind because circumstances have changed or you are in possession of more information. You do not have to defend your decision to other people.

■ **You have the right to be yourself.** Too often people try to live their life by other people's standards, to comply with the social norm. You can choose where you live, who you live with (or not), where you work, how you spend your personal time, hobbies, interests and so on.

BEING RESPONSIBLE

I said at the start of this chapter that sometimes people wrongly describe someone who is being aggressive as being assertive. Assertiveness isn't aggressiveness. We've looked at asserting our own rights and it's important to balance those with two important responsibilities.

▓ **It is vital to respect other people's rights.** The rights you take for yourself, you should give to others. For example, you should allow other people the right to refuse, not to consider their own needs or to make a mistake. Turning this around, the rights you give to others you should take for yourself. For example, if you give others the right to change their mind, to not assert themselves or to be themselves, then you need to take these rights for yourself.

▓ **Accepting our rights needs to be done in a reasonable and responsible way.** You will only make life more difficult for yourself if you defend your rights at all times. For certain minor issues you can choose not to assert yourself; you have the power to do this. For example, if a customer is giving you a hard time over some small issue that is clearly their fault. You do not have to assert yourself – as long as this is a conscious decision made from your thinking programme and not a submissive one. We all have the right to make mistakes; however, it's important to admit our mistakes, either to others or to ourselves, and ensure that we learn from them and don't repeat them. It is important to allow other people to make mistakes, without humiliating them and making them feel bad.

If we want to be assertive, we must:

▓ Openly express how we feel.

▓ Give and take fair criticism.

▦ Make a decision about what we want.

▦ Decide if it's fair.

▦ Ask clearly for it.

▦ Be calm and relaxed.

▦ Be unafraid of taking risks.

However, we must not:

▦ Bottle up our feelings.

▦ Go behind people's backs.

▦ Beat about the bush.

▦ Bully people.

▦ Call people names.

▦ Ignore our own needs.

YOU CHOOSE

Let's look at some examples of conversations. Write beside each comment whether it is submissive, aggressive or assertive. The answers are below.

1   You are about to face a difficult person and a colleague says:

a) 'You better stand up to her. Don't let her browbeat you into doing what she wants.'

Behaviour: _____

b) 'If I was you, I would just keep my head down and listen to what she says. It'll probably make things worse if you try to argue with her.'

Behaviour: _____

2   Your manager asks about a presentation you've just given to a new customer that hasn't gone well and you say:

a) 'It was a total waste of time. You didn't tell me that it would be mainly staff attending and not decision makers.'

Behaviour: _____

b) 'I didn't prepare well enough. I didn't expect the decision makers not to attend.'

Behaviour: _____

3   You're about to leave the office to visit a client and a colleague asks, 'What time will you be back?' You say:

a) 'When you see me!'

Behaviour: _____

b) 'I'll be back at 4.30.'

Behaviour: _____

4   Your manager compliments you on a presentation you've just given to a client and you say:

   a)   'I was really nervous. I always find these things really difficult and I'm sure I could have done better.'

   Behaviour: _____

   b)   'Thank you!'

   Behaviour: _____

5   You phone a supplier's salesperson to thank them for lunch and to apologise for being late and you say:

   a)   'Thank you for the lunch and for explaining about your new product. I apologise for being late.'

   Behaviour: _____

   b)   'Thank you for the lunch. I'm sorry I was late – I'm so busy nowadays it's difficult to get to appointments on time. Sorry I wasn't able to hear more about your new product.'

   Behaviour: _____

The answers are:

   1   (a) Aggressive
        (b) Submissive

   2   (a) Aggressive
        (b) Assertive

3   (a) Aggressive

(b) Assertive

4   (a) Submissive

(b) Assertive

5   (a) Assertive

(b) Submissive

It's not a case of any of these being good, bad, wrong or right. It's primarily about the subconscious messages you send out to other people. When we looked at the programmes of behaviour, we considered how one programme could invite another. If people subconsciously sense that you are submissive, which comes from your passive programme, this could invite aggressive behaviour from them. For example, in 4(a) above the manager may start to think:

'I thought she did okay in the presentation, but she's a real pain. If she feels so bad about it, I'm not going to ask her again in case she makes a mess of it.'

It is also the case that people often don't realise that their behaviour is aggressive. Let's imagine, for example, that a manager says to a member of his team:

'You're a real genius with PowerPoint. Could you finish this presentation for me? I know you're busy, and it might keep you late, but it won't take you that long.'

This is aggressive behaviour because it's manipulative. The manager is not considering the rights of the team member; he is only concerned with his own interests. This could invite aggressive or submissive behaviour (defiant, controlling or passive) from the team member. They may say or think to themselves:

a) 'Why does he always pick on me to do this? It's not fair – I've got a life outside of this office.' (Submissive)

b) 'If he thinks I'm doing this again, he can get lost. It's his job not mine and there's nothing in it for me.' (Aggressive)

None of these responses contributes to a healthy office environment. They potentially make the manager's job harder, create more stress for everyone and generate *more difficult people.*

ASSERTIVENESS TECHNIQUES

There are several techniques you can use to respond assertively in a difficult situation. The first one is:

Broken record

This comes from your thinking programme. It is the skill of being able to repeat over and over again in a calm, relaxed and assertive way whatever it is you want or need. This continues until the other person concedes or agrees to negotiate with you.

I recently bought a small number of items at my local supermarket. When the lady at the checkout asked me for £8, I handed over a £20 note. She gave me change for £10 and handed me a £2 coin. I said:

'I gave you a £20 note, so I need another £10 please.'

She replied with:

'Are you sure? I think it was £10.'

'No, it was a £20 note so I need another £10 please.'

'But I've shut the till now and I can't open it until I do another transaction.'

'I understand; however, I gave you a £20 note so I need another £10 please.'

I was under a certain amount of pressure at this moment because there was a queue behind me and people had their shopping on the belt. The checkout lady said:

'I would need to get a supervisor to come and check this and these people would have to move to another till.' (More pressure)

I said:

'It would be good if you get a supervisor because I gave you a £20 note, so I need another £10 please.'

The supervisor arrived and she explained how the till couldn't be opened. I repeated my request using the same words in a calm and relaxed tone. The supervisor said:

> 'We'll check the till at the end of the day and, if it's £10 over, we will contact you. Can you give me your phone number please?'

I replied:

> 'I understand why you would want to do that; however, I have just given this lady £20 and she has given me change for £10 so I need another £10 please.'

Eventually the supervisor instructed the checkout assistant to open the till and give me my £10. She said:

> 'We will still need your address and phone number.'

I said:

> 'No problem, here are my details.'

I never heard anything again from this supermarket.

When I tell this story to the participants in a seminar, I can see some people starting to squirm. Do you remember what you read earlier about the five factors of success? The fifth factor is courage, and you will need this to stand up for your rights. I wasn't becoming irate or angry – I wasn't being unpleasant to the supermarket staff. I just wasn't leaving that supermarket without money that was rightfully mine. You can use the broken record technique to:

■ Stand up for your rights.

■ Stand your ground.

■ Say what you want or how you feel.

Negative assertion

This technique is used primarily to deal with criticism from a difficult person. Again, this comes from your thinking programme. This is where you calmly agree with the true criticism of your negative qualities.

Let's say a colleague turns to you at work and says:

'Your desk is a real mess – there are papers everywhere. How can you work in a mess like that?' (Controlling programme)

You might reply:

'It's not that untidy and anyway I've been very busy. I've not had time to keep it tidy.' (Passive programme)

As you now know, this response in this situation will invite controlling programme behaviour from your colleague and they will say:

'You should make more time to keep it tidy – it looks terrible!'

It would be far better for you to respond to the initial statement with:

'I agree, it's untidy.'

This is what we call negative assertion. If you use this response, there is not much else the other person can say. They may come back at you with:

'Well, why don't you tidy it up then?'

If you reply:

'You're right, it does need to be tidied up.'

they'll probably give up and go away. Remember, you have the right to have an untidy desk if you want.

This isn't fight or flight; it's often described as verbal judo. As in judo, you use the other person's strength and roll with it. If you're happy to accept that you have certain faults and are not perfect, people will be less likely to put you down.

It may be that you wish to agree with only part of what the other person is saying. This is sometimes known as **selective agreement**. Say, for example, a customer was berating you:

'You people are absolutely useless. I've been waiting two weeks for my order – you never deliver on time.'

An assertive reply would be:

> 'You're right – two weeks is a long time to wait for your order.
> What I'm going to do now is _____ '

In this situation, you are only agreeing to the part of the statement that says: 'I've been waiting two weeks for my order.' You are not agreeing or attempting to defend the part: 'You people are absolutely useless' or 'You never deliver on time'.

Let's look at another technique.

Fogging

You would use this technique to deal with manipulative criticism and to defend your self-esteem. Fogging is about agreeing in principle and staying out of it emotionally. You are paraphrasing and reflecting back what the other person has said into more rational, factual and less emotive terms. It is responding from your thinking programme, not reacting in an emotional manner.

There may be some truth in what the difficult person is saying, but they may elaborate or exaggerate. For example:

> 'Your report is late again. You have no consideration for
> anybody else – you don't care if this makes life difficult for me.'

The fact here is that the report is late; all the other stuff is emotional. The temptation in this situation is to react to 'You have no consideration for anyone else' and 'You don't care'. If you attempt to defend yourself, it's possible you'll reply in a submissive way:

> 'I've been up to my eyes in work. I've tried my best to get this done on time. I do care about making life difficult for you.'

It is far better to ignore the other person's emotional remarks. Instead, respond in your thinking programme and reply assertively:

> 'Yes, it is late again and I apologise for making life difficult for you. I'm obviously not planning my time correctly – perhaps you could help me.'

Don't be concerned if you're confused by the differences in these techniques. As long as you grasp the basic principles of:

■ Staying out of it emotionally.

■ Having confidence in yourself.

■ Believing in your right to be untidy or make a mistake.

■ Always responding from your thinking programme and communicating assertively.

THINK ASSERTIVELY

Do you remember the story I told you earlier about a farmer who wanted to borrow a portable milking machine from his neighbour? He wound himself up into such a state beforehand that he abused his friend immediately he opened his mouth. Sometimes, when managing a difficult person, it's easy to react emotionally and not think things through.

Imagine you have to manage a difficult colleague and your thoughts go something like this:

> 'When I try to discuss this problem with Bob, he'll fly off the
> handle and we'll end up in a shouting match.'

If that's what's in your head, what do you think your resulting behaviour will be with Bob? It's very likely to be aggressive or submissive; you're either going to end up fighting with Bob or trying to pacify him.

An assertive approach would be:

> 'When I discuss this problem with Bob, I will calmly present the
> facts. He may get angry and start shouting and, then again,
> he may not. If he does I will tell him how I feel about the
> situation in a calm and controlled manner. I will ask him why
> this situation has occurred and ask for his thoughts on how we
> can resolve it. I will not react to any emotional statements from
> Bob.'

Here's another example of your thoughts before a meeting with Mary:

'I'm not going to enjoy this. When I tell Mary that her sales are not good enough, she'll probably burst into tears just like she does with everybody.'

How do you think you might approach the situation with Mary? I suspect you may be submissive or even aggressive. An assertive approach would be:

'When I speak to Mary, she may burst into tears or she may not. Whatever happens, I will calmly explain why I am not happy about her sales results. I will listen to what she has to say and ask her how I can help. If she does become emotional and start to cry, I will empathise with her and continue to offer help and support to improve her sales.'

Assertiveness is a very positive response in any interaction. It makes it clear to the other person what you're unhappy about and allows you to state your case calmly. It in no way affects their human rights.

6

The Power of Persuasion

'Not brute force but only persuasion and faith are the kings of this world.' – Thomas Carlyle (1795–1881, Scottish philosopher and author)

DEVELOPING YOUR SKILLS

This is probably the most important chapter of this book because in order to get what you want out of life – to be happier, to have better relationships and to master the ability to manage difficult people – you need to be better at persuasion.

As I said in Chapter 1, interaction with other people is the most important factor in your life. Even if you wanted to, you would probably find it difficult not to have to deal with other people. You possibly want to live with another person, to get married, to have children, to have friends and to work with other people. Yes, there are exceptions to the rule: some people prefer to live on their own, work on their own and have as little contact with other people as possible. However, for the majority of us it is vitally important to have positive relationships with other people. If you ever find yourself on a deserted beach somewhere and other people show up, I bet they come and sit beside you.

Your relationships, as well as giving a great deal of happiness, can also cause unhappiness and negative stress. You find yourself having to persuade other people to accept your point of view, your product or service, your proposal of marriage or your ideas and beliefs. The challenge is: other people don't always wish to be persuaded by you. It may even be wrong to attempt to persuade them. How many times have people been persuaded against their will or better judgement to do something that they later regret?

I believe, however, that it is vital to be better at persuasion. After all, think of the instances when your power of persuasion is in the other person's interest. It could be far better for the other person if you persuade them to:

■ Give you a job.

■ Stop smoking.

■ Eat their vegetables.

■ Take a holiday.

■ Buy your product or service.

■ Marry you.

■ Lend you money (think of the interest they'll earn).

There are many situations where your power of persuasion has benefits for the other person as well as you. In any persuasion process you're looking for a win–win outcome. This is where you benefit as much as the other person. If this is not the case and it's a win–lose situation, then instead of persuasion you may be talking about manipulation, control or coercion. However, as any good salesperson or negotiator knows, a win–win outcome is what you should always be aiming for.

'Everyone lives by selling something.' – Robert Louis Stevenson (1850–95 Scottish essayist, poet, novelist)

I will always remember the first sales course that I ever attended, and the definition of selling that was drummed into my brain:

'Selling is the art of creating a desire in the mind of a buyer and satisfying that desire so that the buyer and seller benefit.'

That may seem a bit old-fashioned for many of today's salespeople, but I believe the principle still holds true. You no doubt have noticed that I have started to talk about salespeople and buyers. This is because I believe that we are all salespeople and buyers from the moment we enter this world.

A baby crying for food, attention or a change of nappy is trying to persuade you to take action. If you don't respond to this initial request, then they step up the volume until you do. Because you love that child, because you care, you are very open to that persuasion. So it follows throughout your life – if people care about you, if they respect you, if they have good rapport with you, then they are more likely to accept what you're proposing.

The sales or persuasion process is very much part of our world. It is often far better to sell than to tell. A manager will frequently get much further with the people who work for him or her by selling rather than telling. If staff can understand the benefits for them, then they are more likely to respond in a positive manner to those who supervise them.

> '*You can get everything you want in life if you'll just help enough other people to get what they want.*' – Zig Ziglar (1926–, American author, salesperson, motivational speaker)

The sales persuasion process starts very early in life – in fact, children are often very natural salespeople. They persuade their parents to do all sorts of things:

> 'Dad, if you buy me these running shoes, then I will win all the races at school and think how proud you will be of me then.'

> 'Mum and Dad, if you buy this computer for me, then you'll be able to use it also.'

> 'Mum, if you buy this multi-vitamins cereal for me, think how pleased you'll be when I grow up big and strong.'

They may not be using these exact words but you can see the win–win scenario:

'If you give me this, then think how good it will be for you.'

We are more likely to respond to this type of persuasion rather than:

'Buy me these new shoes because I want them' or 'Buy me this computer because it's the latest model.'

My friend Susan was telling me recently about Ben, her three year old. Ben loves boats and ships. While out shopping together, Ben spotted the ex-Royal Yacht *Britannia* tied up at the dockside in Leith, Edinburgh. His request:

'Please can we go on the boat, Mummy?'

was initially turned down by Susan. He then said:

'If we go on the boat, Mummy, you could have a nice cup of tea.'

Ben has already learned that selling is more likely to get him what he wants rather than a straight request.

As we grow up, the sales process continues in a very natural way. Picture the husband saying to his wife:

'That car of ours is starting to cost us a lot of money in repairs. I'm often worried that it will break down when I take you to work. That touring holiday we had planned may have to be cancelled.'

Or the wife to her husband:

> 'Have you noticed that your shirts are not as clean as usual?
> That washing machine seems to use a lot of electricity. I think
> that the spinning action is damaging your clothes.'

These are two classic sales situations. The husband is trying to persuade his wife that they need to buy a new car, and the wife is working on a new washing machine. They are both unconsciously using the pain or pleasure principle. We tend to move away from situations or things that cause us pain, and towards things that give us pleasure. In both of these scenarios, both parties are outlining the pain that is, or will be, unless their sales pitch is accepted.

So, whether we like it or not, selling and persuasion is going on all the time. Marketing experts believe that we all receive about 3,000 sales messages each day. There are all the obvious television and radio advertisements, the billboards, bus and train advertising, newspapers and magazines. Think for a moment of all the people who walk about advertising products – their clothes and footwear display names and logos that indicate how successful or trendy they are, or how much street cred they have. Companies such as Nike, Adidas, Tommy Hilfiger, Gucci and many others have learned the value of selling their brand.

As well as all the obvious commercial products and services, think of some other things that are sold, such as politics and religion:

'Vote for me and I will improve your quality of life.'

'Come to my church and your spiritual life will improve.'

Many of the products and services, ideas and philosophies that we've been sold, have enhanced our lives. If we hadn't been sold them, do you think we would have tried to seek them out? I don't think so. It isn't enough to invent or develop something – it needs to be sold. I can imagine the person who tried to sell the first fax machine met a lot of resistance. How do you send a fax to another person who doesn't have a machine? Persuading people to climb into the earliest aeroplanes and fly across the Atlantic also took some selling.

As Thomas J. Watson (1874–1956), the founder of IBM, once said:

'Nothing happens in this company until somebody sells something.'

Many positive things have taken place in human life because somebody persuaded others to do or accept something; unfortunately there have also been many negative things. Adolf Hitler sold the German people many propositions that could enhance their lives. Many Germans bought into his philosophy in a classic win–lose situation. The 'product' that Hitler was selling just wasn't right and ultimately proved to be disastrous for the German people. In the 1960s many pregnant women were sold the idea of taking a sedative drug called thalidomide. As you know, this led to the birth of children with malformed limbs. Again, the product wasn't right.

People tend to remember the times when they were sold or persuaded on something that turned out not to be right for them. This gives the whole area of selling and persuading certain negative connotations. However, it's important to remember that many, many positive outcomes have taken place from either a product, a service or an idea being sold. If you develop your selling and persuading skills, then you are going to have a better job, a better standard of living, better relationships and a happier life. It is going to make it much easier to manage difficult people.

It is worthwhile considering your natural attributes as a persuader and looking at how you can enhance them. Many of these attributes lie dormant in your subconscious. You can, with a little thought and a little application, develop your power of persuasion.

IT'S ABOUT CHANGE

Persuasion is about change, and what do you think the majority of people feel about change? That's right – they don't like it! The majority of people in this world are resistant to change. They fear it, seeing it as a threat rather than an opportunity. Can you imagine the boss walking into your place of employment one morning and announcing: 'We're going to make some changes around here.' Isn't it the case that almost everyone becomes uneasy and views the aspect of change as something to fear?

If you're going to persuade someone to change their behaviour, viewpoint, attitude or any other aspect of their business or personal life, then you're talking about changing a mindset. If anyone is going to change their mindset, then they need to envisage benefits for them that outweigh their present circumstances or situation. If you're the person doing the persuading, then you need the skills, qualities and characteristics that make you believable and credible.

Credibility

When I was a teenager, I always remember my mother saying: 'Don't let me catch you smoking cigarettes – it's bad for your health!' Of course, at the time, my mother and father both smoked and it didn't appear to do them any harm. Credibility is only one of the qualities you're going to need if you want to be a successful persuader. Let's consider some of the others and how we develop them.

Belief

Successful persuaders believe in themselves and what they're talking about. After all, if you don't believe in what you're saying, how do you expect anyone else to?

Enthusiasm

I've known people who believe in what they're saying but fail to communicate with any enthusiasm or passion. Many people find difficulty with this; however, if you want to persuade someone, get enthusiastic about it.

Knowledge

You need to know what you're talking about so make sure you have all the information, facts, figures and statistics.

Empathy

Put yourself in the other person's shoes – what do you think is important to them? Consider why they should accept what you are saying. If someone is really frightened of flying, then there's no point telling them not to be silly and to stop behaving like a baby. You need to consider how you might feel and what might persuade you to change your mind if you were in their position. You need to outweigh the fear with benefits.

Persistence

If you want to persuade someone, don't give up on the first 'No' or any sign of rejection. Persist and persist – but nicely. People won't necessarily react in a negative way to persistence when they realise that you really believe in what you are saying. There is a line you can step over, so be very careful. Watch the other person's reactions and, if it's apparent that you're persisting too much, stop!

Energy

Put energy into all your interactions with other people – energy fuels enthusiasm. We are persuaded by people with energy. Many television presenters use their energy to sell us their ideas. When I was a child there was a scientist on television who persuaded us that science was interesting by waving his arms about all over the place and getting very excited. He was the original mad professor but you certainly listened to what he was saying.

Consistency

Everything you do or say is important – everything counts. If you want to be a successful persuader, then you must be consistent. If you're trying to persuade someone to keep their promise, then you must always keep yours. If you say: 'I'll phone you back in ten minutes', then you must phone back in nine minutes. If you're persuading someone about politics or religion, then you must consistently live by those philosophies. Business leaders who preach restraint on wage demands lose credibility if they drive large cars, live in large homes and fly by private jets.

To be a successful persuader, you need many skills, qualities and characteristics. Even with these all in place, there is still no guarantee of success. However, people are more likely to be persuaded by others whom they trust, like and have a good relationship with.

USING LOGIC AND EMOTION

When we make a decision about something, do we do it logically or emotionally? Hard as it is for many people to accept, we allow our emotions to rule our decision-making process. Research conducted at Harvard Business School some years ago discovered that 84% of buying decisions were made for emotional reasons. Many sales and marketing people will argue that 100% of buying decisions are made for emotional reasons and then justified logically.

Take, for example, the motor car industry. The majority of cars nowadays have efficient engines, comfortable seats, many safety features, air bags, stereo equipment, air conditioning and so on. Picture the man or woman who buys the BMW, Mercedes or Jaguar. The features in all of these cars can also be found in a top-of-the-range Ford or General Motors car. Why then do people pay so much more money for the BMW, Mercedes or Jaguar? Is it prestige, status, a desire to impress the neighbours or just because they always wanted that car? This is a purely emotional decision, but you'd probably find that the buyers of these cars would argue the logic of spending the extra money.

Advertisers are particularly aware of the power of emotions. A few years ago British Telecom ran a successful advertising campaign in the UK featuring that little person from outer space: ET. Not much mention of all the logical telecom products and services that they supply but definitely an ad campaign to pull at the heartstrings!

Manufacturers are very much aware of the value of their brand in terms of sales and profits. At my local health club the majority of members wear expensive, branded training shoes. We all know that training shoes purchased in a cut-price shop would cost so much less and do the same job, but do you want to be seen wearing them? I don't think so. There are many people who make logical decisions when buying a product or service. These are the people who buy the cheaper training shoes, shop in the cut-price store and who wouldn't be seen dead in designer clothes. However, isn't that in itself an emotional decision?

The lesson is that, if you want to persuade someone, if you want to sell them an article, service or idea, then you need to appeal to their emotions.

Left brain or right brain

In 1981 Roger Sperry and Robert Ornstein won a Nobel Prize for research into the brain. They established that there is a left brain and a right brain, and that they perform different functions. The left brain is the logical half and the right brain the more emotional half.

The left brain deals with:

- Words

- Numbers

- Lists

- Details

- Logic.

The right brain deals with:

- Pictures

- Colour

▪ Imagination

▪ Space

▪ Rhythm.

Because most of us have had primarily a left-brain education, it is natural for us to communicate in a logical manner. From day one at school, you learned the three Rs: reading, writing and arithmetic. In history class we were taught to remember dates, in geography we learned details of every country and in science we learned even more facts. Our childhood was full of facts and figures. Only, possibly, in the music room or the art class were we allowed to use the right side of our brain.

When we communicate with other people, we tend to believe that if we give logical reasons then the other person will be persuaded. The problem is, of course, that the person we are trying to persuade is often using both sides of the brain, and in the decision-making process the right side, the emotional side, is more dominant. If the person you're trying to persuade doesn't like the colour of your tie, the colour of your skin, your monotone voice or the size of your body, then there's no way they're going to listen to your logic.

My mother, who died a few years ago aged 89, always had a problem with men who wear earrings. I think she believed that only pirates wear earrings and, of course, they are not very nice people. If a man wearing an earring tried to sell my mother something or persuade her in some way, I am sure she would view him as some relative of Captain Blood. The logical side of her brain just wouldn't engage; she had all the wrong pictures in her mind.

It has to be said, however, that some people are more logical than others and always let their head rule their heart. I've worked with engineers and people in similar technical jobs, some of whom have great difficulty in coming to terms with the whole right brain, emotional thing. When they find themselves in a sales situation or when they need to persuade someone about their product or service, they often come unstuck. They believe that, if they give the specifications of the product, show the test results, quote a competitive price and a fast delivery, then they will get the order. They fail to realise that their scuffed shoes or unkempt appearance may work against them.

Toupee or no toupee

During a seminar the managing director of a printing company told me that he'd recently had a visit from a sales engineer selling printing machinery. This was only one of many times they met to discuss the purchase of highly technical and expensive machinery. My friend, the MD, told me that when he sat in his office talking with the sales engineer he couldn't help noticing his toupee. The thought that kept running through his mind was: 'You're pretending that you're not bald – what else are you pretending about?' The sales engineer did not realise that his structured and logical persuasion process was being sabotaged by an ill-fitting hairpiece.

So, whether you like it or not, if you want to be persuasive you need to remember that you're communicating with a person, not a robot. Powerful persuaders always appeal to the right side of the brain more than the left. Appeal to the other person's emotions and you are more likely to be successful.

Pain or pleasure

Always remember that people will move towards things or situations that appear pleasurable and away from things that will cause pain. If you are trying to persuade someone to eat less, don't tell them that they'll eventually look like a big fat pig. That is a far too painful picture for them. They will shut that picture out of their mind and totally disregard anything you say. It would be far better to tell them that, if they eat less, then they'll look fabulous in their clothes or their swimsuit. That's a far more pleasurable picture to paint for them.

If you want your children to do their homework, don't go on at them about failing their exams, about not going to university and being unable to get a decent job. Talk to them about all the things that are important to them and how they will achieve them with good exam results. Always talk about pleasure not pain – we shut out pain and we don't listen.

> 'The only way on earth to influence the other person is to talk about what he or she wants and show them how to get it.' – Dale Carnegie (1888–1955, American trainer, author)

The feel good factor

Trying to convince someone, to persuade or to sell a product, service or idea can be extremely difficult. However, it will be very much easier if you keep in the forefront of your mind that this is a psychological process. Success is highly dependent on influencing emotions.

People have likes and dislikes, wants and desires. If they're going to make a decision about something, typically something new to them, then they want to feel good.

When you find yourself on the receiving end of a persuasion process, before you buy an idea, new product or different way of doing something, you will make one big emotional decision:

'Do I buy the person who is trying to persuade me?'

Many people in sales or management, or in any other daily interaction with other people, fail to realise the importance of their own personal impact. Quite simply, if you want to persuade someone to change their mindset, to buy a product or service, then you must first sell yourself.

SELLING YOURSELF

Think about a product or service that you've bought in the past. Was it the logical or reasoned argument or the proposal that the person put forward that helped you make your decision? Or, how much were you influenced by the actual person?

A friend of mine recently bought a new car. Before making this fairly major purchase, she assured me that she would visit all the showrooms, looking for the best deal. A few days later I met her with her shining brand-new car. My obvious question was:

'Did you get a good deal on the car?'

'Absolutely,' she replied. 'I paid a really good price. The salesman was such a nice man, I really liked him.'

It then became apparent that she had visited only one car showroom and had been so impressed by the salesman and how she had been treated that she didn't visit any other car dealers. It was obvious that the salesman had made such an impression that she more or less accepted the first deal she was offered. Now, I am not suggesting that she didn't get a good deal. However, I do know that she bought the salesman before she accepted his offer.

Sad to say, confidence tricksters are very aware of this situation. They know that, if they can sell themselves, then people will accept almost anything they say. There are numerous stories of people being sold something that either didn't exist or was never for sale. There is the famous case of an American who paid a con man a great deal of money for Tower Bridge in London. That was definitely not for sale!

Before you can persuade anyone to your way of thinking, you need to sell yourself. Here are six steps to success:

1 First impressions are vital

Most people are aware of this – nevertheless, they still fail to do anything about it. They seem to think that other people will like them better the more they get to know them. This can often be true; however, humans make very fast initial decisions about each other and we tend to stick by these decisions. We make approximately eleven subconscious decisions about other people within the first six seconds of meeting them. This is one of our inbuilt programmes, which helps us to survive.

In a confidential survey conducted with personnel managers they admitted to making up their minds about an interviewee within the first 30 seconds of meeting them. This decision was made mainly on the visual impression. It therefore follows that we must pay a great deal of attention to how we dress, our posture and eye contact, and what we say when we first open our mouths.

Always dress in a way that is appropriate for the impression you wish to make. Avoid dressing in a way that contradicts what you are saying. If you are off to see the bank manager about a loan, then dress as he or she would: look businesslike. If you're about to meet with an angry customer or an upset member of staff, make sure you look smart and professional. This obviously doesn't mean you need to dress like a teenager in order to communicate with one. However, be very aware that all of us, and some more than others, are highly influenced by what we see in other people.

2 Smile

If we want someone to buy us and accept what we say, then they need to feel comfortable and happy with us. A pleasant and genuine smile initially relaxes the other person, even though they may be angry or annoyed. I meet many people in business who have stern, sometimes frightening or even bland faces. They initially make me feel uncomfortable, and if I feel that emotion then I am not totally receptive to what they say.

Smiling is also good for you – it sends endorphins, the happy hormones, coursing around your system. It follows that you need to look after your teeth and your breath. I met someone recently who was most pleased to tell me all about himself. The only problem was that I couldn't concentrate on what he was saying because of his bad breath. People are more likely to say 'Yes' to someone they like the look of, someone with an open happy face and a pleasant smile. Of course, a happy smiling face wouldn't be appropriate when you're in front of an angry or upset customer.

3 Shake hands

Do it positively, firmly and in conjunction with a smile. Don't do the bone crusher – all that says is that you are a bonehead. Some people say that they wait for the other person to offer their hand. If you both stand about waiting, it never happens. Touch is very powerful; it helps create the initial bond. Offer your hand every time you meet with someone you want to persuade or influence. Here's a tip that will tell you whether the other person is resistant to you or not. As you shake hands slightly turn your hand in a clockwise direction. If you feel resistance from the other person's hand, it suggests that they are possibly tense in your company and may initially resist what you say. If their hand turns with yours, it suggests that the person is more relaxed.

Some people, particularly politicians, favour the two-handed handshake. This may be a bit over the top for you, so here's another tip that can help you make an impression on other people. As you shake hands, touch the other person's forearm with your other hand. Do this quickly but firmly, and do it each time you meet this person. It helps to anchor positive feelings about you with the other person, and marks you as someone different.

4 Use positive opening words

After you have made a great impression with how you look, your friendly smile and your memorable handshake, don't blow it all by saying the wrong thing. People tend to believe what they see, more than what they hear, but saying something inappropriate or unclear can spoil the whole self-selling process. The trick is to plan or at least think about what you are going to say before you meet someone. I accept that not all meetings with other people are planned; however, even for impromptu encounters with other people you should have a stock of opening statements and questions. If you are visiting the bank manager or your boss, possibly someone who works with you, or even your child's school teacher, then you should have carefully prepared opening words.

It's a good strategy to get them talking as soon as possible, so keep your opening words brief. For example:

'Hello, John, you're looking well. Tell me, how did you enjoy your holiday in Florida?'

'Good morning, Mr Smith. I really like the design of this office – is it comfortable to work in?'

'Hello, Mary, you're looking well! Have you been taking more exercise recently?'

'Good to see you, Jack. I like your new car – what's it like to drive?'

When you are selling yourself, your opening words need to be positive, genuine and invite a response. It is also very important to use the other person's name, but don't overdo it.

A few years ago I spent a disturbed night in a hotel in Aberdeen. (I always seem to have problems with hotels.) When I was checking out, I asked to speak to the manager. I was tired and grumpy and I wanted to tell him all about his noisy hotel. I was pacing up and down the reception area, building myself up to tell him what I really thought. This smartly dressed man approached me across the lobby, held out his hand, gave me a big smile and said:

'Good morning, Mr Fairweather. My name is Alistair McDonald. I'm the General Manager and I'm pleased to meet you. I'm disappointed to hear that you've had a disturbed night – please tell me exactly what happened.'

I was so taken aback by his positive and friendly approach that I lost most of the energy that I was about to put into my complaint. His thinking programme approach changed me from defiant to thinking mode. I found it hard to be angry and I explained my situation and listened to his apology.

If he had approached me and said something like: 'Hello, I'm the manager. How can I help you?' then he would probably have received a much harder time from me.

It never fails to amaze me how some people, when they meet someone else, say negative things such as:

'My goodness, you're fairly putting on the weight!'

'Hey, John, you're not looking too well – have you been sick?'

'Hi, Bob, are you wearing that tie for a bet?'

The people who say these things fail to realise the effect they are having on others. They then wonder why their friends or colleagues are so unreceptive to what they say. You want the other person to accept you and accept what you say. It is therefore vital to make them feel good and in a positive frame of mind.

5 Be a great listener

This is the most important factor in selling yourself. Many people believe that in order to sell themselves, to make an impression on other people, they need to talk about themselves. All of us have met these people either at work or socially. They tell you all about themselves, what they do for a job, their qualifications, what car they drive, where they go on holiday, who they know, how clever their children are, and lots more. This information is often related very subtly and often can be imparted in one sentence:

> 'We love to holiday in Tuscany because that was where I met my husband the year he finished medical school and I completed my Ph.D.'

> 'Because our daughter has to travel around the country winning even more riding events, we had to buy a Range Rover to carry all her tack.'

This is not the way to sell yourself and certainly not the way to start a persuasion process. The steps to super self-selling are:

- Ask questions.

- Listen.

- Look like you're listening.

Good listening skills have two main benefits:

1   You find out lots of things about the other person: how they think, what they feel and what's important to them.

2   You indicate to the other person that you think they are important, that what they say is important and that you value them. If people get this message from you, then they will buy you in a big way.

As I said earlier, listening is the most important skill if you want to persuade people and deal with difficulties and objections. I make great emphasis of this when I run sales training programmes. So many salespeople want to talk and talk about their wonderful product or service. I encourage them to listen and listen, if they want to be successful. It is so important that I suggest you digest the following points very carefully.

Look like you're listening. Use lots of open body language. Stimulate the speaker by leaning forward, maintaining good eye contact and nodding your head. Change your facial expression relative to what is being said – show your feelings to the other person. Women are fairly good at this; most men are not so good. Men tend to listen impassively, most likely taking it all in, although the message received by the other person is:

> 'You're not listening to me, you're not interested, you don't care and you're thinking about something else.'

It's so important to get this right, particularly when you're managing a difficult person. If they think that you're not listening, you're not interested or – worse – you don't care, then you are in even more trouble. So, as well as all the open body language, make sure you say the occasional:

> 'I see' – 'Really!' – 'Uh-ha' – 'Wow!'

Keep your brain in thinking programme. Many people allow their own feelings or perceptions to interfere with what they are hearing. They listen through filters based on how they see the world. I used to have an aunt Molly, my mother's sister. When I was a child and she came to visit, she would always ask me:

'How are you, Alan, are you keeping well? Are you enjoying school?'

I would say something like:

'I'm really well, Aunt Molly, and I'm enjoying school.'

I would then overhear her saying to my mother:

'I don't think Alan is too happy. He doesn't look too well to me and I think he might be having problems at school.'

For reasons known only to her, and which I still can't figure out, she was telling my mother untruths. It was probably based on how she felt as a child and how she hated school. Her mind wouldn't allow her to believe that I could be happy and enjoying school.

It can be very difficult to keep an open mind and really listen to what is being said to us. We all have these filters in our subconscious through which incoming information travels and is adjusted to suit our understanding. We are all different in how we view the world – so, if someone is telling you something, switch off the filters and keep thinking.

Write it down. It looks professional, it gives the impression that you're interested and it obviously gives you a record of what was said. I've found myself in the situation where I'm making some points to another person and they're just looking at me. I've sometimes said: 'Do you not want to write this down?' and they reply: 'It's okay, I'll remember.' This does not give me a good feeling!

Look them in the eye. I used to work in an open-plan office and, although I had a small screen between myself and everyone else, I used to get distracted very easily by the slightest thing. If I had an important telephone call, I used to cover my eyes to stop myself being distracted by something or somebody else in the office. When I find myself in a face-to-face conversation, I have to concentrate very hard and resist the temptation to look over the other person's shoulder.

You don't have to stare at the other person but it's important to keep good eye contact, only looking away briefly and occasionally. In Chapter 3, we looked at the five factors of success. Under the section on rapport, I talked about NLP and how it can help your communication skills. NLP teaches us about eye movements and how we can gain an insight into what people are thinking.

In the simplest terms, if a person is looking up to their left as they speak to you it means they are remembering a particular situation. If they look up to the right, it means that they are constructing a situation. In other words, they may be telling a lie. Practise this with your friends (without telling them of course) and watch those slight eye movements they make as they tell you a story. Are they flicking up to the left or up to the right? And I hate to tell you this, but if they are left-handed the eye movement interpretation is the other way round.

Ask the occasional question. It helps your understanding and tells the other person that you're interested in what they're saying. Sometimes it is useful to paraphrase and repeat back what the person has just said:

> 'What you're saying, Mr Smith, is that this product is too big for your purpose.'

This can also help you to take control of a conversation with a difficult person who may be talking too much.

Concentrate on the tone of voice. As you're no doubt aware, a person's tone of voice determines the meaning of what they're saying. We're all fairly good at picking up on a person's tone of voice, but it's still important to concentrate on the sometimes subtle changes in tone. If you're managing a difficult person and you say: 'Are you happy with my suggestion?' and they reply: 'Yes, I'm happy with your suggestion', make sure they sound happy before you continue.

Listen with your eyes. The first thing you notice about another person is their attitude. When you come face to face with a difficult person, you don't need to be a genius to work out that they're angry or annoyed. On the other hand, body language signals can sometimes be very subtle so it's important to keep your eyes as well as your ears open. Remember what I said above about eye movements. Observe all the non-verbal clues and listen for what people are not saying, or are having difficulty putting into words.

Don't interrupt. When people are speaking, there is a great temptation to jump in with an answer or a solution to the problem. Please resist that temptation.

6 Talk about the other person's interests

Do you remember back in the dark ages before digital cameras and you had to wait for your holiday photographs to come back from the processor? All those happy snaps of friends and family, people you met on the beach, places you visited. Who is the first person you look at in these photographs? You might hate to admit it, but you know that you'll always check out yourself. 'I look good in this one.' 'This picture doesn't flatter me.' 'I look too fat in this one.'

We are the most important people in our universe. We worry about how we look, how we sound and how we are perceived by other people. Our self-image is the most important thing in the world to us. That is why so many people fear standing up and speaking in public. We feel that our self-image will take a pounding. People won't like the way we speak, the way we look and they'll make us very aware of this by laughing at us.

If we want to sell ourselves and become expert at managing difficult people, then we must continually boost the other person's self-image. When we talk to them, it must be in terms of their interests, not ours. Many people fall into the trap of talking too much about themselves.

I love the story related in Michael LeBoeuf's book *How To Win Customers and Keep Them for Life*. He talks about a young lady, recently married and explaining to her friend why she had married Bill instead of Bob.

'Bob is everything,' she said 'handsome, well educated, extremely intelligent and has a great job. In fact, when I'm with Bob, I feel that I'm with the most wonderful person in the world.'

'Then why did you marry Bill and not Bob?' her friend asks.

'Well, when I'm with Bill, I feel like I'm the most important person in the world.'

When we are self-selling, we need to talk to people about the things they are interested in. If you are trying to persuade them, talk about how they will feel. Don't say:

'I would be really happy if you did what I suggest.'

Do say:

'Think how happy you will be if you accept my suggestion.'

When someone tells you about their holiday in Florida, don't say:

'I've also been there and I loved Disney World and the Everglades, and we went to some fabulous beaches and we had a great time!'

Do say:

> 'I've been there too. What did you enjoy most about your
> holiday?'

It's really quite simple stuff, yet so many people fall into the
trap of talking about themselves rather than the other person.

If you want to be interesting then be interested!

These are the six steps of self-selling that will help you sell
yourself and ultimately help you manage a difficult person
and sell what you're proposing. Remember:

People buy people first, and they buy people who are like themselves.

The successful persuader will spend most of their time
building a close relationship with the other person. They will,
however, put their point across and ask the other person to
accept it. How you put your point across and how you ask
someone to accept it is what we're going to look at next. We
will also look at the fact that people may resist what you say,
and how you deal with that.

PLANNING YOUR STRATEGY

You may feel that it isn't always possible to plan or prepare
what you are going to say to people, particularly in day-to-day
situations. It is important, however, to have some guidelines
or a model that you can fall back on for these interactions. In

many situations where we need to use our persuasive skills, there is the opportunity to plan. If you were about to:

▦ have a meeting with a difficult person

▦ go for a job interview

▦ persuade someone to do something for you

▦ sell your house

▦ deal with someone who works for you

or any of the multitude of other interactions you have, being prepared will increase your chance of success in getting someone to accept what you say.

When planning you need to consider the following:

1 What do you want from this meeting? Write it down and be clear in your own mind. Also consider what your fallback position would be. What would you be prepared to accept? What concessions will you make?

2 What are you going to say? Again this needs to be written down, choosing the words carefully. We need to think more in terms of questions rather than statements and we'll consider this in more detail later in the chapter.

3 What will they say? Think carefully about any resistance that they might offer and what you will say in return.

4   How will they react? Will they be pleased, unhappy or angry? Will they burst into tears or just laugh at what you say?

5   Do you have all the information you need? Are there any facts and figures you'll need? Is there anything you want to show the other person?

6   Are you psyched up for this meeting? Are you in a positive frame of mind expecting a positive outcome?

Being prepared will give you more confidence in any interaction and increase the likelihood of your success as a persuader.

THE INITIAL APPROACH

If you know the other person and have previously made a good job of selling yourself, then you should experience a positive response when you initially approach them. If you don't know them so well and they don't know you, then the steps of self-selling come into play. Selling yourself is not a long process. Human beings make decisions very quickly about other people, so remember the six steps:

1   First impressions are vital.

2   Smile.

3   Shake hands.

4   Use positive opening words (use names).

5   Be a great listener.

6   Talk about the other person's interests.

Remember, these six steps will influence everything you say. I've said it before and I'll say it again:

'If they don't buy you, then they won't buy what you say.'

So let's look more closely at what you do say when attempting to get your point across.

WIIFM

'If you would persuade, you must appeal to interest rather than intellect.' – Benjamin Franklin (1706–90, American scientist, publisher, diplomat)

The above acronym is found in most sales books and, although it looks like the name of a radio station, it does in fact stand for: 'What's in it for me?' I like to think of it as a radio station, running a regular programme in everyone's subconscious mind. Whenever someone makes a suggestion to us, tries to sell us something or attempts to persuade us, WIIFM switches on. This may appear selfish but it is just the way people are. We are concerned about what the other person is proposing and how it will affect us. When you put your point across, talk in terms of what's in it for the other person because they also listen to WIIFM.

Don't say: 'I need you to help me tidy up this office.'

Do say: 'Would you be willing to help me tidy up this office and make it more comfortable for us to work in?'

Don't say: 'I want you to do some overtime.'

Do say: 'Would you be prepared to do some overtime and receive time in lieu?'

These examples may seem simplified and would need to be tailored to suit each situation. The principle, however, is not to talk about what you want but rather how the other person will benefit.

Also, whenever possible make your point in terms of a question rather than a statement. If you were trying to persuade your partner to take you on a holiday, rather than saying:

'Let's go on holiday and enjoy some sun, a nice beach and some sightseeing.'

it would be far better to say:

'When we go on holiday, which would you prefer: the beach, the swimming or the sightseeing?'

Posing a question causes the other person to really think about what you've said because they know they need to answer you.

Professional salespeople are aware of WIIFM and consider it when making a presentation. The jargon that they use is called 'features and benefits'. You don't talk about what your product or service does, you talk about how the potential customer will benefit.

Don't say: 'This television comes with a Dolby pro-logic six-speaker surround sound.'

Do say: 'Mr Smith, when you watch and listen to the football on television, would you like to feel that you were actually at the game?'

Don't say: 'This bed has a firm mattress and a reinforced base.'

Do say: 'Mrs Brown, would you like a good night's sleep and relief from your stiff back?'

Don't say: 'Fill in this form and you'll get some compensation.'

Do say: 'If you are willing to complete this compensation form, you will be able to replace what was damaged with brand-new items.'

Too often people make statements and expect the other person to work out the benefits for themselves. The problem is that they don't! And if they do, by the time they have worked it all out they've stopped listening to you.

So many times when interviewing someone for a job, I've listened to them talk through almost everything that is on their CV:

'I have a degree in English.'

'I have attended several sales training courses.'

'I have experience in various industries.'

'I obtained all my Boy Scout badges.'

Rarely did I find an interviewee who related his or her skills and experience to what I wanted in the job and I often found myself saying internally: 'So what!' That little radio station, WIIFM, was playing in my subconscious. This may seem harsh or unkind when someone is using all they know to get an important job. I always tried to treat job applicants with respect and in the interview steer them towards talking about benefits. Sadly this rarely happened and it's one of the reasons I started writing this book.

People in their everyday lives are trying to persuade other people on issues that have many benefits for both of them. The problem is that the person doing the persuading is more often than not making a poor job of it. Now that I've got that off my chest, let's look further at how we become better persuaders.

DEALING WITH RESISTANCE

We all know that most often when we try to persuade someone they resist what we say. In selling we call these 'objections'. Dealing with objections is what selling is all about and sadly too many salespeople do it poorly. If you believe in something, if you think of a great idea, if you really like somebody, then you probably get frustrated if other people don't feel the same way. The obvious reason that they don't feel as you do is that they are not you and they have a different view of the world. It's important to let them know that you understand their situation and that you always talk in terms of their interests. Only in this way are they likely to accept what you say.

Why do we get resistance?

Let's consider all the reasons why people would resist what you say. As I have already stated, other people have a totally different rulebook on life than you do. However there are some other specific reasons.

They don't like you. Now, it may be that they don't dislike you – it's just that they haven't bought you. You haven't done a good enough job of selling yourself.

They don't trust you. Again it comes down to self-selling. People will base their level of trust in you on the smallest incident. For example, you promised to phone them on a Monday morning but didn't do so until Monday night. You don't think that that's such a big deal, but it could be a big deal to the other person and could influence how much they trust what you say.

They don't understand. People often say no to something, basically because they don't understand what you are talking about. They may question you to clarify what you are saying, but more often than not they won't. Asking you to explain is often too much trouble for some people. They also feel that they may come across as being stupid. It's far easier just to say 'no' to what you are suggesting.

They didn't listen. One of the main reasons why people resist what you say is that they haven't really listened to what you said. This is different from not understanding; they just haven't taken in all the information from you or picked up any of the benefits of your suggestion. The reasons people don't listen are numerous and take us back to the listening skills that we considered previously. I believe that very few people listen well when someone is speaking to them for a number of reasons:

▨ They are distracted by someone or something else.

▨ They're tired or bored.

▨ They're in a hurry.

▨ They think they know what is being said.

▨ They daydream.

▨ They don't understand your jargon.

▨ They're physically uncomfortable, too hot or too cold.

▨ They are thinking about what to say next.

People are either speaking or preparing to speak. The point, of course, is that if people have not listened they won't necessarily admit to it – they just reject what you say.

They really don't want what you're proposing. For reasons known only to themselves or for reasons they may tell you, people may not be interested in what you are saying. For example, if you tried to persuade me to go to the opera I wouldn't go. You might think it's wonderful but I've tried it and I didn't like it.

A difficult person may not want what you're proposing. Sometimes it's best to ask:

'What can I do that will make this right for you?'

Remember: whenever you're trying to persuade someone or when you're trying to sell them something or bring them round to your way of thinking, you won't win them all.

They don't want it now. Sometimes people may be fairly agreeable to what you are proposing, but they don't want to do it now. The person you've asked to marry you may say 'No' but maybe later things will change. Don't give up but maybe just put it on the back burner to simmer for a while.

They don't like change. Human beings are creatures of habit. We live and work in little comfort zones. We get up in the morning, have the same thing for breakfast, take the same route to work, do the same job, and then come home and watch the same TV programmes. We then get defensive if anyone or anything tries to change any of these situations. Remember what I said previously about humans being totally driven by their emotions. Change is a very emotional issue. If you and your partner have enjoyed going to the same hotel in Spain every year for holidays, then trying to persuade him or her to go somewhere else could be difficult. You may have all the logical reasons in the world why you should holiday in Greece, but they just won't accept them. Resistance to change is often the most difficult resistance to overcome.

'Any change, even for the better, is always accompanied by drawbacks and discomforts.' – Arnold Bennett (1867–1931, British novelist)

All of this resistance can be difficult to handle and, as I said previously, you won't win them all. However, by using some simple techniques, you can win more situations. It has to be said that dealing with people and trying to persuade them is not about getting the better of them. In any persuasive interaction you should be aiming for a win–win situation. If you aim for a win–lose situation, you will only do it once because the other person will never be persuaded by you again.

Before we look at resistance-handling techniques, consider the fact that there are basically two types of resistance: logical and emotional. If you refuse your 17-year-old daughter's plea for a first car, then you may respond logically:

'You don't have the money to buy and run a car and you've no way of finding it.'

Or emotionally:

'You're much too young. I didn't get a car when I was 17 and I'll never know where you are.'

When you're trying to persuade someone, it's important to identify quickly whether their resistance is logical or emotional. The easiest way to do this is to ask questions. They may be saying one thing, but they may mean another. In order to uncover the real reason for resistance, you need to ask questions such as:

- 'What makes you feel that way?'

- 'What makes you say that?'

- 'Is there something about what I've said that you're uncomfortable with?'

Direct but respectful questioning is more likely to uncover the real reason for resistance. Say, for example, you're dealing with a difficult customer and they say:

'I'm not accepting your offer of compensation – you can just forget it!'

Perhaps they mean:

'I haven't understood a word you've said.'

Good questioning will uncover the real reason why the customer is refusing your offer, and then you can deal with that.

Eight steps for dealing with resistance

1 Listen. When the other person resists what you say, use all of your listening skills. Let them finish what they want to say – don't jump in with a question or a counter response.

2 Be attentive. Look like you value what they say. Use lots of positive body language and good eye contact.

3 Pause. When the other person has made the point, pause for two or three seconds. It gives you time to think and it suggests to them that you are carefully considering the position.

4 Compliment. It may be appropriate to say:

'That's a very good point' or 'Thank you for raising that.'

5 Ask. This is where you need to check for understanding. Do you have a logical response or an emotional one? You might ask:

'What part of what I've suggested are you unhappy with?' or 'If you can't help me now, when do you think you will be able to help me?'

6 Empathise. This may seem a strange thing to do; however, it isn't about agreeing with someone but more about understanding how they feel. You could say:

'I understand what you mean' or 'I appreciate that you feel this is a big job.'

7 Answer. This is where you respond using the benefit applicable to the other person – remember: WIIFM. Using empathy you could say:

> 'I understand that you don't want to do this presentation at this time. If you do decide to do it, it will build your confidence and help your promotion prospects in the future.'

> 'If I was in your position, then I would also think I was inexperienced for this job. Would you agree that my youthfulness, enthusiasm and energy more than compensates for my lack of experience?'

8 Check. After you have answered the other person's resistance, check that they are happy with your response:

> 'Are you happy with that?'

> 'Does that make sense to you?'

> 'Do you feel better about this?'

If the person says 'No' and raises more resistance, then it may be appropriate to restate the benefits or introduce new ones. Remember: always answer with benefits that are relevant to the other person – not to yourself!

When dealing with resistance it's not imperative that you use all of these steps; however, the basic rule is empathise and respond with a benefit:

> 'I understand how you feel and what this means to you is . . .'

Other methods to deal with resistance

If you know the other person and are fairly sure what sort of obstacles they might raise, then you may want to bring up the problem yourself:

> 'You probably feel that I don't have the skills and experience to do this job; however . . .'
>
> 'I expect you believe I have no right to ask this; however . . .'
>
> 'You may think this compensation is unfair and I can understand that. Let's consider what this entails . . .'

Be very careful about raising resistance yourself. It only works if you are sure that the other person is about to raise it. If not, you may be planting some seeds of doubt that the other person hasn't even thought of.

Another technique that you can borrow from the professional salesperson is:

Feel – Felt – Found

Again, it is an empathy and benefits response:

> 'I understand how you feel. Your colleague John felt the same way when I asked him. However, what he has now found is that this new system has reduced his workload.'

When you have successfully dealt with resistance, there is one final step you need to take as a powerful persuader. You need to: **Ask!**

'If you don't ask, you don't get.' – Mahatma Gandhi (1869–
1948, Indian political and spiritual leader)

Some people make a fairly good job of handling resistance
and outlining the benefits for the other person. However, they
often fail to ask for what they want or want to happen next.
The interaction is often left hanging in mid-air:

'I know you will really enjoy working in this new department –
there are more opportunities for someone with your skills and,
of course, there's the extra money.'

After making this statement some people just leave it at that,
expecting the other person to respond. What often happens is
that the other person comes back with more resistance to your
suggestion or they just procrastinate. Finish off the above
statement by saying:

'When would you like to start?' or 'Shall I phone the
department manager and tell her you'll be over on Monday?'

Sometimes you can offer an alternative in your closing
statement:

'Do you want to start the new job on Monday, or would you
rather wait till the end of the month?'

'Will you work late tonight or is tomorrow better for you?'

In the world of selling, these statements are known as closing
the sale. For many salespeople, this is the most difficult

part of the job. The reason it's so difficult, and why many salespeople feel uncomfortable about it, is that we hate the word 'No'. Even non-salespeople avoid asking for what they want because they hate to hear 'No' or 'I don't want to' or 'I'm not interested'. The problem is that we take this rejection personally. We think: 'You don't like me' or 'You think I'm a fool' or 'You've got something against me'.

'No' is a form of resistance and, as we saw earlier, it could be said for several reasons. It could be because they don't like you; however, in most cases it will be for many other reasons. For example:

- What's in it for them?

- They haven't understood.

- They really don't want what you're proposing.

- They don't like change.

- They didn't listen.

Whenever you hear the word 'No', don't take it personally. Refer back to your resistance-handling skills and deal with it. As Mahatma Gandhi said, 'If you don't ask, you don't get.' Asking isn't about pressurising someone or being manipulative; it's about being assertive and making it clear to the other person what you want. If you think about it, many people want you to make their minds up for them. They want to be encouraged to buy that new car, to go on holiday or to apply for the new job. So don't let them off the hook – always remember to ask them for what you want.

PRINCIPLES OF A POWERFUL PERSUADER

Prepare for each contact. Always plan for any meetings where you know all your skills as a persuader will be required. It is also good practice to prepare now for any future situation where a detailed plan would be unsuitable. Consider in your own mind how you might handle ad hoc interactions.

Always have a positive objective. Be clear in your own mind exactly what you want from any interaction. Write it down.

Sell yourself. Always remember that if people don't buy you then they are unlikely to buy what you say. Build trust, use names, and smile, be happy and interested in the other person.

Talk results. When making your point to the other person, always talk in terms of results for them. Remember, they are not interested in what you want but, rather, what's in it for them.

Deal with resistance. Don't take it personally and don't argue. Agree, empathise, ask questions and respond with results and benefits.

Ask for what you want. If you don't ask then you might never move forward. Remember, the other person may be quite happy if you help them make a decision.

At the start of this chapter, I made the point that the power of persuasion is important to your happiness and wellbeing. It is not about getting your own way; it is not about manipulating people. It is about bringing other people around to what you believe and in a manner that is beneficial to them. We tend to believe that our own way is best, and that everyone should think like us. However, experience tells us that this is not always the case. This should not stop you from trying to persuade other people that what you say could be in their best interests. It is important, however, to respect the other person's viewpoint and to try to see the situation as they see it. I wish you every success as a powerful persuader.

Strategies for Success

You've no doubt gathered from the preceding chapters that our own behaviour has a huge influence on the number of difficult people we may have to manage. However, I like to think that I live in the real world. I realise that no matter how nice a person you are, or how well you sell yourself or communicate from your thinking programme, you'll still find yourself in the situation of having to manage a difficult person. So you need some skills and techniques you can use on a day-to-day basis. We'll look, initially, at how you might manage a difficult customer or client. Then we'll look at how to manage a difficult member of your team. Of course, these skills can be used to manage almost anyone who is proving to be difficult. You can even use them with your boss!

WHAT CUSTOMERS REALLY WANT

Before we look at some techniques for dealing with difficult customers, it's important to be aware of what they really want in the first place. Satisfying those basic needs will minimise the number of difficult customers you ever have to deal with.

What customers really want can be divided into two areas.

Firstly, they want the core service of your business to meet their needs. They expect your product or service to work. If you say you're a plumber, then the customer expects you to fix their leaking pipe. If you say you're an accountant, then they expect you to resolve their tax details.

They also expect your product or service to represent value for money. If I buy an expensive pair of winter boots I expect them to keep out the cold and wet and also look good. Naturally, if I were to buy a cheaper pair I wouldn't expect them to last as long.

Customers also expect your after-sales service to be efficient. If my new winter boots start to leak when I wear them for the first time, then I expect the shop to replace them immediately.

However, none of this will make customers loyal or cause them to tell others how good you are. They take this core service as a given. You wouldn't see me running around telling people that my new winter boots didn't leak.

Secondly, and this is the most important point, what customers really, really, really want and what will make them loyal to your business and say wonderful things about you to other people are:

■ **Warm and friendly responses.** When customers make contact with you face to face or over the telephone, they want a warm response. It can still be businesslike but you and your people need to look and sound friendly and likeable.

▓ **They want to feel important.** They know that you have lots of other customers and clients but they just love it when you make them feel special.

▓ **They want to be listened to.** Customers often get the impression that the person dealing with them is not really listening. You must keep working on your listening skills. Keep good eye contact with people and concentrate on what they're saying. Keep an open mind and resist the temptation to jump in with an answer. It's also important to show that you're listening. Open body language and head nods when face to face – lots of 'Uh-has' over the phone.

▓ **Someone to know their name.** A person's name is one of the sweetest sounds they'll ever hear. If you use a customer's name when you talk to them, it indicates that you recognise them as an individual. Don't use it too often as it can become irritating, but definitely at the start and the end of a conversation.

▓ **Flexibility.** Customers hate to hear 'No' or 'It can't be done'. It's not always possible to say 'Yes' to a customer or do exactly what they want, however it is important to be as flexible as you can. Tell customers what you can do, not what you can't.

▓ **Recovery.** When things go wrong, customers want you to solve their problems quickly. They don't want to hear excuses or who's to blame or why it happened, they just want it fixed fast. Customers will often judge the quality of your service by the way you recover. They will even forgive your mistakes if you recover well.

Say, for example, you served a meal that wasn't cooked properly or wasn't hot enough. You would need to apologise, show the customer that you care, assure them that it will be fixed and then do it quickly. Tell the customer that they won't be charged for the main course or give them some wine or a free dessert. Then when that customer talks about your restaurant, they'll tell people:

'There was a small problem initially but, when I pointed it out, they really moved themselves and they couldn't have been more apologetic.'

Don't be afraid when something does go wrong; it's often a great opportunity to show customers just how great your service really is.

Overall, customers just want to feel good. They want to feel better after they've dealt with you or anyone in your business than they did before. If you can create that feeling, then you're well on the way to giving customers what they really want and minimising the number of difficult customers you'll ever have to deal with.

Sad to say, some organisations make life really difficult for themselves. Most of the time, it's because their core service lets them down and they fail to provide an acceptable product or service. Nonetheless, they are often let down by poor interactions between their customers and their staff.

Before making a recent overseas trip, I phoned the two banks that I normally use. I wanted to inform them that I might use my Visa debit cards in Singapore and Vietnam. When I telephoned the first bank to tell them this, the customer service person said:

> 'You can't use your debit card overseas, but I'll phone your branch and tell them to allow any transactions.' (Did you notice the two words to avoid?)

He then went all in to ask me some security questions such as the address of my branch and my telephone security number. I explained that I did all of my banking over the internet and that I didn't know the address of my branch or my telephone security number. He asked me a couple of other questions and then informed me, in a very official tone of voice, that I had failed two out of three of his questions and that he had to inform security. I was starting to get annoyed mainly by his tone of voice and his accusing manner. I eventually became so irritated that I told him to forget it, and that I wouldn't use my debit card. This customer service person had just created a difficult customer!

I phoned the second bank with the same information and the conversation went like this:

> 'I want to use my Visa debit card when I travel to Singapore and Vietnam later this month.'

> 'Certainly, Mr Fairweather, I will contact your branch and tell them your plans. Can you please confirm your bank account number and sort code.'

After I'd given him the required information, he said:

> 'Have a good trip, Mr Fairweather. I hope all goes well for you
> and thank you for calling.'

I've had problems with the first bank in the past. But it's never about core service issues; it's always about the interactions I have with people in the bank.

No matter how good your service, it's inevitable that you will have to manage a difficult customer at some time or other. So let's look at some techniques.

DEAL WITH THEIR FEELINGS – DEAL WITH THEIR PROBLEM

If you're faced with a customer who is emotionally charged up, you first have to manage these emotions before you can deal with the problem. In other words, deal with their feelings and then deal with their problem. Many people, particularly in customer service or management jobs, tend to go straight into problem-solving mode and don't attempt to deal with the other person's feelings.

Say, for example, a customer phones and says:

> 'I'm really fed up with you people – you never get anything
> right. That's the third time this month my delivery has been
> wrong!'

What many managers and customer service people say, and it's the wrong thing to say, is:

> 'Sorry 'bout that, give me your account number and I'll sort it out.'

They go straight into problem-solving mode and the customer continues to rant and rage. They believe that if they do something about the problem, or are seen to be doing something, then the customer will calm down. What you really need to do is defuse the customer's anger, and you won't do that effectively by just trying to sort the problem.

Do you remember what we said about interacting on a human level and a business level? You interact on a human level to deal with the feelings, and the business level to deal with the problem.

I used to run customer service workshops for telecom engineers. One engineer was talking about a difficult customer he had to deal with. He was working at this particular customer's house and he inadvertently reversed his van over her prize flowerbed. The customer was obviously annoyed and I asked the engineer what he said to her:

> 'Sorry 'bout that, I didn't see the flowerbed. It's company policy that you have to fill in a form if you want compensation.'

I asked the engineer what happened next and he replied:

'She went crazy, getting even more annoyed. It was a lot of fuss over a few flowers – it's not the end of the world.'

Bearing in mind what you've read so far, you'll recognise that the engineer:

- Didn't see it *how the customer saw it*.

- Didn't communicate on a *human level*.

- Used *words to avoid*.

- Talked about *company policy*.

And he wondered why the customer was so upset!

I asked the engineer to put himself in the customer's situation. I asked him how he would feel if he'd spent a lot of time tending the flowers in his garden and one day a van totally destroyed his pride and joy. How would he feel if someone told him he had to fill in a form? I think the engineer eventually got the point.

Let's consider what he could have said:

'I apologise for destroying your flowers, Mrs Smith. If I had a garden I would hate this to happen to me [human]. Would you be willing to complete a form that will make some contribution towards the loss of your flowers? [business]'

It's unlikely that the customer will magically turn into a meek little lamb when they hear this. But they're more likely to become less difficult if they feel the engineer really cares about the mistake he's made and is apologetic.

You're probably thinking that it's unlikely you'd ever hear a telecom engineer using these words. However, by using his own language and a human response before a business response he could make his life so much easier. By dealing with the customer's human needs, you're more likely to get to the business part much quicker and solve the problem.

Let's look at some other techniques for managing a difficult person.

REFLECTIVE LISTENING

It's sometimes the case that a person, customer or colleague interacts with you out of their passive programme. They are not in controlling or defiant programme but if they're not handled well then they definitely could be. You would use the reflective listening technique if someone were confused, concerned, worried, frustrated or just upset. You wouldn't use it if the other person were really angry and behaving from their defiant or controlling programme. The main objective here is to deal with the customer's feelings and get more information. Once you have done that you can deal with their problem.

Let's say a customer contacts you and says:

'I'm really concerned that the cheque I sent to you doesn't

> appear on my statement. I know I sent it before the due date,
> and I hope it hasn't got lost in the post.'

Think for a moment about how the customer must be feeling
and reflect back that feeling. You could say:

> 'It sounds as if you're worried about getting behind with your
> payments.'

The customer may confirm that they're worried or they may
come back with:

> 'I'm not worried, but I just don't want to incur any late payment
> charges.'

The customer will get the subconscious message that you are
a caring person because you recognise their concern. It's not
enough to look concerned; you have to say something. When
the customer realises that you are a caring person, you'll get
the business part resolved much quicker. Again, if you fail to
address the human aspect, the customer could continue to
whinge and complain and become even more difficult.

USING EMPATHY

We've touched on this before – it's an excellent technique for
defusing a difficult person's problem behaviour. The difficult
person may be in controlling or defiant programme but by
empathising you remain in thinking programme. This has to

be an absolutely genuine response. If you try to fake it, the other person will realise and you'll end up with an even more difficult person.

Do you remember what I said about tone of voice and body language? This isn't about agreeing with the difficult person's situation; it's about accepting that their feelings and opinions are okay for them. Use language such as:

- I understand that you're upset.

- I realise that you are concerned.

- I understand why you would think that.

- I appreciate what you're saying.

- I know what you mean.

Here are some examples:

1

'You promised you'd phone me back and you haven't done so.'

Empathy response: 'I can appreciate that must be very frustrating.'

Saying that is a whole lot better than a passive programme reply such as:

'I'm really sorry. I haven't had time to phone you back as we're very busy at present.'

That will invite a controlling or defiant response such as:

'If you're busy, you should get more staff.'

2

'Have a look at my account. It's much too high – I don't normally spend as much as that in a month.'

Empathy response: 'I can see what you mean. It does seem a lot for one month.'

That is far better than a controlling response such as:

'This system doesn't make mistakes, so if that's what it says then it must be right.'

This may all seem quite simple, but I would ask you to listen to the other person's response the next time you express your concerns about something. I would suggest that in most cases they will go straight to the business part of the problem, without any human response whatsoever. Just think about how you feel in that situation.

Of course, it's not all bad news. There are people who naturally respond in a human manner before dealing with the business. I once had my wallet stolen including all my credit cards. I had stupidly left my briefcase, containing my wallet, in the training room at a hotel where I was running a seminar. As you will understand, I was none too pleased when I discovered the theft and I was angry and annoyed, mainly at my own stupidity. I phoned the company that my credit cards are registered with and gave my name and account number to the person who answered the phone. She replied with:

> 'You must be very annoyed, Mr Fairweather. I'm sorry that this has happened to you. Before I take any details, can I just check – are you all right?'

I explained that I was angry and upset, but felt a whole lot better dealing with someone who sounded like they cared. I suppose that if I had spoken to a less human person then I might have given them a bit of a hard time. This woman dealt with my feelings, defused my emotions and then dealt with my problem.

Get on their side

Sometimes it's useful to add another phrase to the empathy response, including yourself in the picture. If a customer was to say:

> 'I hate being kept waiting!'

Before giving a business response such as:

> 'I'll get you the forms in the next few minutes.'

it's far better to give a human response:

> 'I understand how you feel – I don't like being kept waiting either. Thank you for your patience. I will get you the forms in the next few minutes.'

Some people get concerned when using this response, as they believe it'll lead to:

'Well, why don't you do something about it then?'

Yet the majority of people won't respond this way if they realise you're a reasonable and caring person. If they do, then continue empathising and tell the person what you'll do about the situation.

TRANSITION STEPS

Once you have a level of rapport with a difficult person, you can move to the business part of the interaction to solve the problem. Use empathy or apologise, and give information and ask a question. For example:

'It's a real problem trying to speak to someone in your business. You have to wade through that awful menu system you have, and then you have to wait for ages. You're then told that all operators are busy – it's a real pain!'

'I appreciate your frustration and I'm sorry you've had to wait so long [empathy]. This is a busy part of the day for us and we are making every effort to answer calls as quickly as possible [information]. So that I don't keep you waiting any longer, how may I help you? [question]'

Perhaps the customer is in defiant programme, is much angrier and comes back at you with:

> 'Don't tell me I've got to explain all this again. I've been through it a hundred times with all the other people in your organisation!'

You would answer with:

> 'I can understand that you're angry. No one likes to have to repeat themselves [empathy]. If you'd be willing to explain the situation to me, it'll help me get this resolved as quickly and as accurately as possible. Are you willing to do that?'

Reframe

Let's say that the customer rejects the solution that you offer. You can reframe what you say to resolve the situation. When the customer says:

> 'I don't want you to transfer me to someone else. I have been passed around enough – I want you to deal with it!'

You reply:

> 'I understand what you're saying, Mr Smith, I've been in that situation myself and it can be very frustrating [empathy]. In order to minimise the time it'll take to resolve this, it would be best to speak to the person who will be able to answer your question better and quicker than I can [reframe].'

I want to speak to your manager

A difficult customer will often say:

'I want to speak to your manager.'

You may not want them to do that because:

▨ It may make you look incompetent in front of your boss.

▨ You'd have to explain everything to her.

▨ You have all the information needed to solve the customer's problem.

▨ It's your job to deal with the customer's problem.

You could say:

'I understand why you feel that way, Mr Jones, and I'd probably want to talk to a manager myself [empathy]. However, I'd really like to help you, and I have all the information in front of me. So that we can resolve this quickly, would you be willing to give me an outline of the situation?'

VISIBLE–VOLUBLE CONCERN

This is another technique you can use with a difficult person. It's useful when you realise a mistake has been made and that the other person has a right to be annoyed. It's an alternative to saying sorry, apologising or using an empathy response.

Let's take an example. A customer tells you about a situation in which it seems that a mistake has been made. As soon as the customer has finished explaining, whether or not you know for sure that something has gone wrong, you would respond with:

> 'Oh no, that's terrible! I'll follow up on that personally and I'll call you back.'

You could also paraphrase the customer's words in an escalated tone:

> 'You haven't received the paperwork yet? Oh, no!'

Your expression, tone of voice and body language should reflect your concern. You may need to use this response several times when the customer feels that a mistake has been made. This will ultimately have a calming effect on them. If they feel that you're concerned, he or she will feel more confident that the situation will be dealt with. And if you follow up with empathy you can help the customer become even calmer and more reasonable.

Some people are concerned that this response may sound false. However, it won't sound false if it's a genuine response from you. You can't fake it – the customer will realise if you're being false and they'll feel patronised. People in customer service jobs often feel that by making some admission of guilt this kind of response would let their company down. But that's not what you're doing; you are only showing the other person that you care about their situation.

Imagine this situation. A friend phones to tell you that they've been in a car accident and, although they're not hurt, the car is a write-off. Or perhaps they phone to tell you that they're expecting a baby. Your emotional response to this news will look and sound like visible–voluble concern.

I'm sure that when something does go wrong with someone else, and you know it's a genuine complaint, the words you say in your head may be less than polite. This technique is about letting the other person hear and see your concern, but of course without the impolite words!

All of these techniques can be used when managing a difficult person in any circumstance, not just a customer. However, there are some specific actions you can take with a difficult member of staff – so let's take a closer look.

MANAGING DIFFICULT STAFF

One of the biggest challenges for managers is dealing with staff who:

- are negative and complaining

- have a poor attitude

- turn up late and go home early

- do less than their best to help customers

- lose sales

▓ take too many sick days

▓ de-motivate the rest of the team.

Managers continually ask me what they should do to manage difficult staff. Some believe that there's some kind of quick fix, a magic bullet that will solve all their problems. But life isn't like that – managing difficult staff is a daily, ongoing process.

In Chapter 4, we looked at how prevention is better than cure. If you create the right environment for the people that you manage, then you'll minimise the number of occasions when you have to manage a difficult team member. Creating that environment will be much easier if you start to think of yourself as less of a manager and more of a team leader and coach.

What's the difference?

When I ask participants on a seminar: 'Tell me what a manager does. What are their duties?' They usually come up with responses such as:

▓ Planning

▓ Cost control

▓ Resource allocation

▓ Analysing data

▓ Interviewing

- Solving problems

- Dealing with customers

- Other technical duties.

When I then ask: 'What are the duties of a coach?' I hear replies such as:

- Leading

- Motivating

- Listening

- Encouraging

- Identifying training needs

- Communicating expectations

- Believing in their people

- Inspiring

- Winning and getting results.

There are cross-over duties between a manager and a coach, but let me ask you a question: Which role is going to be the most important in achieving your objectives and minimising the possibility of having to deal with difficult team members? Is it a manager or a coach? Now I know what you're going to say: 'My organisation and my boss want me to do all the management things and that's how I spend most of my time.'

But always remember, at the end of the day, you will ultimately be judged on the success of your team, rather than your ability to complete a report on time.

If you want a happy and motivated team who don't whinge and complain, don't take time off work, don't give you too many problems and who generate results for your business, you need to spend a lot more time leading and coaching and a lot less time managing.

SUCCESSFUL LEADING AND COACHING

1 Spend quality time with each team member

You need to get out of your office or up from your desk and spend time in the area where your team member is doing their job. You need to get to know each member of your team better on both a human level and a business level, and they need to get to know you. Successful leaders and coaches know how to do all the human parts of the job and all the business parts. This isn't about prying into the team member's life – it's about showing an interest in the individual, and most people respond positively to that.

If they have complaints, concerns or negative comments, this is the time to deal with them. Spending time and listening will also send the message that you care about them and show that you're there to help with problems, both business and personal. You can communicate expectations, encourage and inspire them to do even better.

2 Give feedback and coach them

You need to tell each member of your team regularly when they're doing well and when not so well. When you see or hear one of your staff doing something you DO like – tell them about it! When you see or hear them doing something you DON'T like – tell them about it. You can then coach them on the job or identify training needs and agree a way forward. Most employees want to know how they are performing in their job; they want to know if they are doing it right or how they could do it better.

3 Believe in each individual

You need to demonstrate constantly to each team member that you trust and believe in them, by what you say, your tone of voice and your body language. They will very quickly sense if you don't trust them to carry out their job and they'll act accordingly.

If you believe that your people are not to be trusted to do their job, that they'll turn up late and go home early, then that is exactly what they'll do. On the other hand, if you believe that your people will do their job well, that they can be trusted to make decisions that are good for the business and that they'll give you a fair day's work, then it is more likely this is what you'll get.

'The man who trusts men will make fewer mistakes than he who distrusts them.' – Camillo Benso, Conte di Cavour (1810–61, Piedmont statesman, premier)

So there you have it. Successful managers know that to get the best out of their people they need to spend less time managing and more time coaching.

However, life is not that easy, so let's take a closer look at the second point above. As you spend time in the areas where your team members are working, you're going to see and hear things that you like. You're also going to see and hear things that you don't like (but let's come back to that.)

THE GOOD NEWS

When you see, hear or are aware of something that a team member does well, you need to tell them about it. It needs to be done *now*, not next week, next month or at the next appraisal. If you delay, it'll have lost its impact and your team member possibly won't remember what you're talking about. This is a compliment or a thank you.

Now I know that some managers still have a problem with this. They seem to think that they're thanking an employee for simply doing what they're paid to do. Well, let me assure you, this is immensely powerful. It will cut down the number of problems you may have with members of your team, reduce negativity and contribute massively to your productivity.

One of the biggest complaints from employees is that they receive no appreciation for the job that they do. We all want acknowledgement, acceptance and a thank you. It's exactly the same in your private life. If you want your children to do well at school, concentrate on what they do well and give them lots of positive feedback. This will encourage and motivate them to do even better and probably improve the subjects they're not doing so well in.

The other benefit to giving positive feedback is that, if you do it regularly, when the time comes to give some less than positive feedback, it is more likely to be accepted. Your team members will see you as a fair and straightforward leader, who always tells them when they're doing well and when not so well. And if you still have any doubts about this, think for a moment about when someone – your boss, a teacher or someone else in your life – gave you some positive feedback. How did you feel, did it motivate you to do even better? I'm sure it did!

'When someone does something good, applaud! You will make two people happy.' – Samuel Goldwyn (1882–1974, American film producer, founder of MGM)

THE NOT SO GOOD NEWS

When you spend time with your team, you'll see, hear or become aware of certain things you don't like or can't accept. So you need to do something about it. There are three things you could do:

▧ Ignore it

▧ Reprimand

▧ Coach.

Let's look at each of these in turn.

1 Ignore it

Many managers ignore poor behaviour from a difficult team member for several reasons:

■ **They don't want the hassle.** They believe it might lead to an argument and the situation might just get worse. It might also cause bad feelings in the team and they'll end up with even more difficult people.

■ **They don't have the time.** This may be a genuine reason, but it's often just an excuse to avoid the hassle. Sometimes a manager feels it's best to wait until the next appraisal.

■ **They hope it will resolve itself.** Perhaps it won't happen again or the team member will just stop being difficult.

■ **They don't know what to do.** Some managers haven't been shown or trained in how to handle a difficult team member. Perhaps that's why you're reading this book.

The consequences of ignoring it are:

■ **The rest of the team becomes de-motivated.** They know what's going on; they can see what's happening. If you don't do something about poor behaviour or a difficult person, then you will lose the respect of the rest of your team.

▓ **Your business is affected.** If you have a difficult or underperforming person on your team, the results are going to suffer.

▓ **The team member continues to behave badly.** They think you don't care and see no reason to improve.

Ignoring a difficult member of your team is not an option, it's an easy way out and it will only make *your* life more difficult.

2 Reprimand

Many managers deal with difficult staff by coming down hard on them. They give warnings about what will happen if they don't shape up. The results of reprimanding are:

▓ **Staff become totally de-motivated.** The team member 'switches off' and just goes through the motions each day. (Have you ever felt motivated after being reprimanded?)

▓ **They spread discontent in the rest of the team.** As well as performing poorly or moaning and complaining to you, they grouse and gripe to the rest of the team.

▓ **They give poor service to customers and colleagues.**

▓ **Your business suffers and, ultimately, you suffer.**

▓ **They might leave.** You may think this is a good thing, but perhaps it may make your life harder in the short term. And you end up having to interview and train a new person.

■ **They improve and stop being difficult.** It is possible, but highly unlikely. They may improve in the short term, but sooner or later they revert to being difficult again.

3 Coach

This is the best option. It is not some kind of touch-feely approach. It's about finding out the cause of the poor performance or difficult behaviour and discussing with the team member how to put it right.

Previously we looked at giving positive feedback. If you've been doing that on a regular basis, then the difficult team member is more likely to listen to what you have to say when the message is not so positive. There are huge benefits to coaching that overcome all the points under ignoring and reprimanding. If you do it well, you will have a happier team member who performs well and doesn't give you a hard time.

HOW TO COACH

■ **Do it now.** Don't wait until the next appraisal – deal with the problem as soon as you become aware of it.

■ **Do it in private.** It makes sense, but often a manager lets his or her thoughts be known in front of the whole team believing that they'll all benefit. Trust me – they won't!

■ **Don't beat about the bush.** Tell them how you feel about their behaviour.

▪ **Don't talk about the company or other members of the team.** You're the manager and it's you the team member has to please.

▪ **Use lots of 'I' messages.** Say things like: 'I just overheard you speaking to a customer and I'm unhappy with the way you spoke to them. I'm willing to hear what you have to say. However, we need to agree on what happens in the future because that behaviour will cause us to lose customers and I'm not prepared to accept that.'

▪ **Be very specific and focus on one thing at a time.** Do not build up a whole list of behaviours that you've previously been ignoring. That is not coaching – it's back to reprimanding and that's not what this is about.

▪ **Be very descriptive about what your concerns are.** Say things like: 'I overheard you speaking to a customer and I heard you say that it wasn't your responsibility and that you couldn't help them. These are not words I want you to say. However, I'm willing to listen . . .'

▪ **Listen to what they have to say.** It's important to get the team member's input. Perhaps they are always complaining about work because they have personal problems at home. It's important that they come up with a solution as to how their difficult behaviour can be resolved. If they don't, you can make suggestions, but you are really looking for their buy-in.

▪ **Don't make it personal.** This can be a challenge, but what you want to do is discuss the person's behaviour rather than their personality. This is not an attack on the person – it's about job-related behaviour. You are not saying: 'You have a bad attitude' or 'You're just a trouble maker' or 'You don't care about anyone but yourself'. As I said before, use lots of 'I' messages and say things like: 'I'm unhappy that your report is late for the third time, John, and I'm willing to listen to what you have to say and agree on how we resolve this situation.'

Believe me, once you start to apply this, you'll make your life much easier, have less stress and more productive employees. Here are some more techniques you can utilise.

USING YOUR CUSTOMER SERVICE SKILLS

When managing a difficult team member, you can use the skills we detailed previously on how to manage a difficult customer. You can use empathy and say:

'I understand that you feel this way. It is difficult in this market to obtain more business and keep customers happy.'

It's important to listen and show that you're listening – you'll gain a much better understanding of each individual on a personal level and how they're handling the job. It may also give you an insight as to why they are negative and always complaining. Some people just like to sound off once in a while, and the mere fact that you're listening can minimise the amount of negativity. It's often the case that they just want acknowledgement as we discussed in Chapter 1.

LOOK FOR THE POSITIVE

This is another way to manage a team member who's being difficult or negative. Try concentrating on what they do well and tell them about it. Look for something positive in what they do, no matter how trivial. There's no need to go over the top but say, for example, they arrive earlier than normal and start working. Tell them:

'Good to see you, Brian. Thanks for starting earlier than normal – I appreciate it.'

Spend less time discussing negative issues or even ignore them. It's not uncommon for managers to invest 90% of their energy responding to negative performance and only 10% strengthening positive performance. Let me give you another example of what I mean.

Treat people like a dog

I know you're going to think I'm a bit mad (probably true) but bear with me on this story.

I really like dogs! I don't have one at the moment because it isn't practical. Whether or not you have a dog, you probably know that it has to be house-trained. As a puppy, it comes straight from the kennels and expects to continue doing its business wherever and whenever it feels like it. So you have the challenging job of training the puppy to do what nature requires, but elsewhere and preferably outside.

I've had four dogs in my time and they all had to be house-trained. I've also observed other people training their dogs. I remember one of my neighbours with his new puppy. Every time the pup did his business on the living room carpet, or wherever, my friendly neighbour would grab the dog and give forth with lots of 'Bad dog, dirty dog' and 'Don't do that again!' Lots of shouting and shaking the poor mutt! The dog, of course, was quickly learning the message that doing the you know what was a bad thing to do. It was okay at the old kennels, but here it was totally different and obviously not acceptable. So it took forever to train the poor dog that it was still okay to do the business, but it had to be done outside.

I, on the other hand, being extremely clever and also wanting to get the whole house-training bit over as quickly as possible, took a different tack. I used to keep a close eye on the puppy and very soon realised when he wanted to go. I quickly scooped him up and headed out the door. As soon as the dog had done what he had to do in the garden, I piled on lots of praise: 'Well done', 'Good boy' and lots of happy noises! The puppy quickly began to realise that, whenever he felt like doing the business, he would get all excited and head for the back door. He knew that this meant lots of good stuff: fun, praise, the occasional chocolate drop and, of course, physical relief.

So what's all this got to do with managing difficult people? Too many managers are spending too much time concentrating on what a team member may be doing wrong. They believe their role is to fix what they perceive to be broken. On the positive side, they may fix the problem with on-the-job coaching or further training. However, many take the attitude that the bad dog treatment will do the trick.

As you spend time with your team, listen to what they are saying and observe what they're doing. When you see or hear them doing something well, give them some positive feedback. As it says in the book *One Minute Manager*:

> 'Catch people doing something right.'

This is not to say that you ignore poor behaviour, but it is more about concentrating on what people do well. Doing this will encourage more of the good behaviour and much less of the poor behaviour. Think: Praise not Punishment!

If you reward good behaviour, you'll get more of it.

If you reward bad behaviour, you'll get more of it.

It has to be said, of course, that some difficult people may not respond to coaching, so here are some further thoughts.

THE TRUTH ABOUT STAFF WHO CAN'T PERFORM

When I started my first job as an apprentice engineer, I quickly realised that some of my fellow apprentices shouldn't be in the job. They just didn't have the aptitude or ability for engineering. Back in those days, and I don't mean Victorian times, staff selection wasn't very sophisticated. All budding apprentice engineers were interviewed by a foreman and, if he liked the look of you, the job was yours.

I was lucky enough to be interviewed by a foreman who, in his spare time, was a captain in the Boys Brigade. I was a member of another BB company so, guess what, I got the job. Neither I nor any of my fellow apprentices were ever tested for our ability, or for any natural talent we might have for engineering. As a result, many apprentices shouldn't have been there in the first place. However, most of them struggled on and qualified as time-served engineers. The problem is they didn't turn out to be particularly good engineers and, I also suggest, they weren't particularly happy engineers.

I've experienced customer service people who shouldn't be let anywhere near a customer, secretarial assistants who couldn't spell or type fast enough, engineers who couldn't read blueprints and plumbers who couldn't plumb.

If you have someone in your team who is unable to do the job and is unable to learn, and is making life difficult for you, then you need to transfer them into something they can do, or advise and help them to find other employment. Now I know that may seem harsh and it's not always easy or feasible to release people; however, you'll never achieve your outcomes with the wrong person in the job. The business may suffer and you're in great danger of de-motivating the other members of your team. They won't want someone on the team who can't do the job.

A client of mine realised that the customer service person they'd recently employed couldn't handle the pressure of difficult customers and situations. They realised that training wouldn't solve the situation, so they transferred her to a job where she produced quotations and didn't have to speak to a customer.

What you need to do is get people who can't do the job into a job that they can do, or get them out of your team.

I joined three companies as a manager and in each case I inherited team members who didn't have what it took to do the job. I'd usually find three categories of people in the teams. The first group were the good guys, the ones who I knew could do the job and wouldn't give me any hassle. The second group consisted of people who needed a bit of looking after, watching closely and definitely some coaching.

The third group were the ones who didn't have either the skills or the characteristics to do the job and no amount of training or anything I could do would change that. I would often find that these people, due to their lack of success, weren't exactly happy in the job anyway and were sometimes only too pleased to be transferred to another position.

I hear you saying, 'Easier said than done, Alan', and you're right. But the successful manager needs to address these issues and bite the bullet for the good of the team and the business.

SUMMING UP

Managing difficult people is a challenge we all face at some time in our life. It may be someone you work beside, work for or who works for you. In your personal life you have friends and family or the people next door, who may on occasion be difficult. I've emphasised throughout this book that prevention is better than cure. If you keep getting toothache, it doesn't make a lot of sense to keep running to the dentist to fix the problem. That causes both physical and financial pain for you. It's far better to brush your teeth twice a day, use dental floss and have a check-up twice a year. Some people, however, perceive that to be just too much trouble and would rather risk the toothache. But by making small changes to your behaviour, they become habits that make your life so much easier, minimise the number of difficult people you have to manage (and stop the toothache).

Choose your behaviour – do not allow other people to choose it for you. Do not allow yourself to be hooked by what other people say or do. Switch to your thinking programme before opening your mouth or taking action. Choose to be assertive when you need to; allowing yourself to be submissive or aggressive will make your life much harder.

Become a powerful persuader by developing your ability to sell yourself. Persuading others involves better listening skills and the ability to communicate on an emotional level.

When faced with a difficult person, be it a colleague or a customer, always be aware that they may see the world differently from you. Empathise with their viewpoint and offer solutions that ensure a win–win outcome.

I wish you every success!

Index

acknowledgement, 23, 24, 198
aggressive, 29, 106, 107
anger, 5, 6
assertive, 106, 107, 117

behaviours, 25, 26, 29, 30, 38
belief, 61, 134
beliefs, 65
body language, 6, 73, 150, 191
Branson, Richard, 59
broken record, 117
bullying, 17
business-level responses, 81, 195

caring programme, 37, 44
change, 25, 133
choice, 47
choose your behaviour, 25, 209
coach, 194, 196, 201
coaching, 195
comfort zone, 65
company policy, 4, 98, 182
conflict, 21
controlling programme, 36, 45, 85, 93, 94, 97
core service, 176, 178
courage, 75, 78, 119
customer service, 20
customer's name, 177

default programme, 34, 49, 51
defiant programme, 36, 44, 85, 97
de-motivating, 207
descriptive, 202
difficult person, 9, 14, 20
dominant behaviour programme, 49

emotional reasons, 137
emotions, 3, 84, 86, 136, 142, 165
empathise, 90
empathy, 135, 184, 187
endorphins, 145
energy, 66, 69, 135

feedback, 196
feel – felt – found, 170
feel good factor, 141
fight or flight, 40, 107
first impressions, 144
fogging, 122
Ford, Henry, 60
fun programme, 34, 42, 102

goals, 62

human brain, 31
human-level responses, 81, 181, 186, 195

jargon, 95

LeBoeuf, Michael, 155
likeability factor, 86
Lincoln, Abraham, 25, 57, 90
listening skills, 149, 177
low self-esteem, 2

manipulative, 7, 9, 35, 93, 122, 172
Maslow, Abraham, 65
mind control, 53
Murray, Andy, 28

negative assertion, 120
negative issues, 204
negative thoughts, 54
NLP, 72
non-assertive, 43
not competent, 22

outcomes, 133, 207

pain or pleasure, 131, 141
passive programme, 35, 43, 67, 96
personal problems, 22, 202
personality, 25, 29, 30
persuasion, 126, 127
pet peeves, 99, 103
poor behaviour, 76, 199, 206
positive opening words, 146
positive performance, 204
prevention, 80
problem-solving mode, 180

quality time, 195

rapport, 70, 72
recovery, 177
reflective listening, 183
reframe, 189
relationships, 11
reprimand, 200
resistance, 162, 163–5, 166, 168
rights, 109, 120
Rosenzweig, Mark, 32
rules and beliefs, 38

sales- persuasion process, 129
selective agreement, 121
self-talk, 55, 59
stress, 8, 22, 127
submissive, 94, 106, 107

team leader, 193
the way it is, 102
thinking programme, 37, 46, 67, 85
tone of voice, 6, 26, 27, 39, 73, 92, 101, 153, 185, 196
training, 61
transfer, 189, 207
trust, 88, 136, 163, 196

warm response, 176
Watson, Thomas J., 132
WIIFM, 159, 162
wrong words, 92

About the author

Alan Fairweather is a dynamic speaker who has been motivating audiences from around the world for more than 17 years.

If you would like to find out more about Alan, please contact him at:

Alan Fairweather International
6 Keith Row
Edinburgh EH4 3NL
Scotland, UK
Tel: +44 (0)131 315 2687
Email: howto@managedifficultpeople.com
Website: www.themotivationdoctor.com

BOOSTER SHOTS FROM THE DOC

Visit Alan's website and subscribe to Motivation Booster Shots. Two or three times a month you will receive a free email newsletter with tips, techniques, skills and strategies for building business. Discover how to motivate your team, motivate your customers and motivate yourself.